A 30 DAY MANUAL TO A DELIBERATE HEALTHIER LIFE

Choice
Driven
Life

BECOME THE COMMERCIAL DRIVER
OF YOUR LIFE

Law Loadholt
Living, Loving, Laughing, and Libations
Foreword by Antonio T. Smith Jr.

C hoice
D riven
L ife

Become The Commercial Driver of Your Life

We will embark on a 30 day journey of Mastering Your Choice. It is time to release complacency and live the highest expression of self. There are 12 pitfalls that will subject you to not Master Your Choice. These pitfalls can also cause friction in personal and intimate relationships.

Copyright © 2022 by Trient Press

All rights reserved. No part of this publication may be reproduced, distributed, or transmitted in any form or by any means, including photocopying, recording, or other electronic or mechanical methods, without the prior written permission of the publisher, except in the case of brief quotations embodied in critical reviews and certain other noncommercial uses permitted by copyright law. For permission requests, write to the publisher, addressed "Attention: Permissions Coordinator," at the address below.

Criminal copyright infringement, including infringement without monetary gain, is investigated by the FBI and is punishable by up to five years in federal prison and a fine of $250,000.

Except for the original story material written by the author, all songs, song titles, and lyrics mentioned in the novel The Silent Wars are the exclusive property of the respective artists, songwriters, and copyright holder.

Trient Press

3375 S Rainbow Blvd #81710, SMB 13135

Las Vegas, NV 89180
Ordering Information:

Quantity sales. Special discounts are available on quantity purchases by corporations, associations, and others. For details, contact the publisher at the address above.

Orders by U.S. trade bookstores and wholesalers. Please contact Trient Press:

Tel: (775) 996-3844; or visit www.trientpress.com.

Printed in the United States of America Publisher's Cataloging-in-Publication data:
Loadholt, Law
A title of a book : CDL- Choice Driven Life

ISBN

Hard Cover	978-1-955198-41-7
E-Book	978-1-955198-42-4
Paperback	978-1-955198-43-1

Table of Contents:

INTRODUCTON
Day 1: How I Could Have Been Complacent
Day 2: Do You See Life As A Learning Experience
Day 3: Are Your Personal Relationships Suffering
Day 4: Never Feeling Nervous or Scared In Life
Day 5: Fear of Change
Day 6: Taking Steps To Improve Yourself
Day 7: Are You Coasting In Life
Day 8: Taking Life And Its Gifts For Granted
Day 9: Are You A Doormat
Day 10: Financial Complacency
Day 11: Physical Complacency
Day 12: Forgiveness: Part I
Day 13: Forgiveness: Part II
Day 14: Set Up New Goals
Day 15: Vision Wall
Day 16: What's Your Why or Reasons Behind Your Goals
Day 17: BYE BYE Doormat
Day 18: Count Your Blessings
Day 19: Self Development
Day 20: Law Of Attraction
Day 21: Law Of Allowing
Day 22: Laws Of The Universe: Part I
Day 23: Laws Of The Universe: Part II
Day 24: The Secret To Life
Day 25: Self Love
Day 26: Complacency With Your Partner: Part I
Day 27: Complacency With Your Partner: Part II
Day 28: Complacency With Your Partner: Part III
Day 29: Complacency With Your Partner: Part IV
Day 30: Wrap Up!
DEDICATION TO MY FATHER

Forward By Antonio T. Smith, Jr.

I met Law at a Les Brown event and we immediately shared energy that would last forever. The first thing we ever did was have a "Who could dress better" contest. He won by a mile. The last thing we did was toss and receive— I tossed him my hat that had "KING" embroidered on it and then walked out of the building into my chauffeured vehicle. Both of these events are exactly why I am writing this foreword for Law. First, because I will never be able to out dress him, so this is my apology for even trying to do so, and second, because I didn't know it then, but I would be tossing him the Paton and he would be taking it further than I ever could.

My name, is Antonio T. Smith Jr, you may have heard of me. If not, you will soon. I am known as a big deal in some business circles, but I could never compare to Law in *any* circle. Law is the most genuine person to ever walk planet earth. He is both master and student— both beginning and end. Somehow, Law walks the fine line of "living all mistakes" and "making all the best possible decisions". And that is Law in a nutshell. He is a man that has lived every single mistake a person his age can live while still having the good harvest of a person who lives a choice driven life.

I am so excited for you to read this book. I read the first version, when it was 60% shorter than what you are holding in your hand now, and it was out of site. This version is more like a sacred text for those wishing to change the quality of their lives.

I challenged law to do a 30 day exercise a few years ago that would push him to the limit of his effort and take him to the precipice of his own destruction. I told him, "Only when man is at the precipice of destruction, does man desire to change." Law, was doing great in life when I told him this and gave him the challenge, but great was not good enough to him. He wanted more. He wanted to be the best. Consequently, I challenged him to a near impossible task. Not only is he the first person to complete the task, he remains only one of two people to ever do it, but he has the most abundant harvest of the two. Law, is clearly not normal. He does not play by our rules and he does not move within our time. He is an enigma.

I believe *Choice Driven Life* is Law's blueprint to teaching someone how not to move within the limits of this world, but to transcend them. There is something special about this book, just as there is something special about Law.

For the next thirty days, give yourself away to this book. Allow the unlimited energy of *Choice Driven Life* to wash over you so you can write your own purpose in life, so that others can stop making you live the life they want you to live. True happiness only comes when someone allows their life to truly be what they create it as.

The primary aim of Law's book is to teach you how to make your own decisions— the decisions that make you the driver of your *own* life. Inner happiness is actually the fuel of this book. Law has it and now Law has packaged it within this book. I pray that this book resonates within your heart. I pray that you follow your bliss and live in the constant space of your joy.

I hope that you become as contagious as Mr. Law Loadholt. I hope that you move into the era of your own choices. Law sees a future of unbounded potential for you. This book allows you to go anywhere, and to do anything. Every great teacher that has come to this earth has shared the same energy as Law. They have breathed the same air as you. According to the *Choice Driven Life,* everything you have encountered has led you to this book. Imagine what you can do from this day forward from what you now know and from the energy this book holds.

I believe you are great. I believe you are like Law. I believe we are one. I believe in you like I believe in Law. That is what I know for sure.

You can plant better. You can dominate.
~Antonio T Smith Jr.

Introduction

According to the dictionary, the word complacent means to be especially pleased with oneself

to the point of being unaware of potential danger. That danger is a lack of passion and purpose.

Your desires create Passion. What do you love? Purpose is the why behind it all. What gets you up in the morning?

We will embark on a 30 day journey of Mastering Your Choice. It is time to release complacency and live the highest expression of self. There are 12 pitfalls that will subject you to not Master Your Choice. These pitfalls can also cause friction in personal and intimate relationships.

I created this book to help rid the world of mindless souls, just wandering around not living up to their highest expression of self. Did you know 97% percent of humans are not living their dreams? That means 3% of the world is controlling and owning up to their abilities.

This journey was inspired by my awesome mentor Antonio T. Smith Jr., who made me dig down deep on what I am willing to die for and what makes my heart hurt. I will die for my nieces and nephews. Complacency hurts the core of my soul. It was time to own up to my choices and create a better life for me.

My mission is to Improve Mindsets and Elevate Vision of Self. Please read this book over a course of 30 days to help you to zero in on your pitfalls and become a greater you. It's time to Release, Reflect, and Renew!

"LIFE IS CHOICE DRIVEN, YOU ARE THE DECIDING FACTOR IN ALL THAT YOU DO." -Law Loadholt

12 Pitfalls Of Not Mastering Your Choice

Day 1:
How I Could Have Been Complacent

Foster Care

Over the course of my life I have heard so many reasons as to why I was taking away from my parents at the age of 3 and placed into foster care. Foster care provides care for children and youth who are not able to live with their biological parents. When parents are unable, unwilling or unfit to care for a child, the child must be placed in a safe place.

Some of the stories that were told where drug abuse played a major factor, child protective services was called by a family member, one parent had a heavier drug abuse than the other, and one parent walked away. Out of all the stories told, my mother paid the heaviest price. She was an officer that lost everything. My father walked away as a result of increased addiction and sought comfort in the arms of another woman.

I am one of eight children; but five of my siblings have experienced the harsh realities of the foster care system and we all have a different story. We spent about six months in foster care and custody was granted to my father. At this time, there were only four of us growing up in foster care and he could only provide for two children. The youngest two were placed back into foster care.

My father raised my brother and I for five years and then he placed us back into foster care. He dropped us off like trash in the night and he never said goodbye. I later learned that he thought he was providing a better life for his children. He was having problems with the new wife and couldn't handle single fatherhood.

During this time, I still didn't know who my biological mother was and it was a process to reunite with her. I am thankful that my mother came back for us (As I type these words, a tear drops from my eyes)! Chances are very slim that a parent regains custody of their child, let alone five. Thank you Lady!

I was a child raising himself in foster care, bouncing from home to home. I was nothing more than a check. There was no one teaching me right from wrong or forcing me to go to school. I can remember many hungry nights and no clean clothes. I would pray that the other foster children would not steal my shoes off my feet as I slept. Somehow there was always a light within me that never dimmed. I would always look to the brighter side for I knew that this wouldn't be my reality forever!

Decline of 23

The number twenty three means new beginnings in the book of life and prosperity in the Asian cultures. My new normal was becoming disabling at 23, unable to provide for myself, and trapped in a world of therapy and an endless supply of medication. I went from college graduate with a promising future to a disabled zombie with over ten grand in debt.

Agoraphobia is a fear of crowds, situations, and the outside world. Panic Disorder is a psychiatric disorder in which debilitating anxiety and fear arise frequently and without reasonable cause. I have always dealt with anxiety, but agoraphobia was a result of getting severely sick after a tonsillectomy and adenoidectomy. This was a routine operation that caused me to be severely sick in the hospital for two weeks. I was unable to keep anything down, high fevers, cold chills, and night sweats. The acid from my vomit was eroding the enamel in my teeth. I went from a size 34 to 27 in two weeks. Keep in mind when you have a tonsillectomy and adenoidectomy you are not allowed to eat anything for one week. I was already losing weight.

The doctor discharged me from the hospital with a clean bill of health, but my psyche was unstable. I became terrified of the outside world and suffered from delirium, which resulted in a deep psychosis. Psychosis is a loss of reality that causes an individual to do and say crazy things. My mother had no choice but to admit me into the psychiatric hospital for treatment.

It was a long journey to become myself again. It was a process to be able to use public transportation and travel on a plane. Yoga was a tool that I used to calm my thoughts and build relationships again. I was able to work a part time job at T-Mobile and build myself up as a productive member of society. These experiences could have caused me to be complacent in life; however I chose to continue to fight. I knew deep down inside of me I was destined for greatness. The sunken place (to better understand watch the movie Get Out, that's how I felt in my psychosis) was not for me.

Reflect~~ Release ~~Renew

Reflect:

What behaviors come to mind after reading this chapter?

_____

_____

_____

_____

Release:

What behaviors are you going to let go of?

_____

_____

_____

_____

Renew:

How are you going to ensure you are not repeating the behaviors you have released?

_____

_____

_____

_____
_____
_____

Day 2
Do you see life as a Learning Experience

Life is a never ending journey of self-exploration. Life has a purpose, and if you do not know what your purpose is; I challenge you to figure it. Find out your strengths and talents and use it to the best of your abilities. While you are on this process you must enjoy and have fun, I promise you the fun makes life a whole lot easier.

To ensure life is a learning experience you must take the time to learn new things for self and/or your career. I rise early every single morning to train my brain into becoming a better entrepreneur and speaker. Name one thing you can do in the mornings to train your brain_____.

I would often practice my Spanish and German in the morning as well. My goal is to become proficient in both languages so I can create content on my YouTube channel in both languages. There are so many free options to learn a new language. My favorite is Duolingo.

When you are not learning you are not growing. Your brain is a special kind of organ that acts like a muscle. It can be trained to improve different cognitive functions like working memory or math skills. Working memory is the reason you can remember a recipe or the process to cook food. I remember that summer I was taking a GMAT class at Baruch College to apply for a Master's Program. It was so exciting to challenge my brain and relive high school math. If you haven't guessed by now I am a bit of a geek! Spoiler alert...I never took the GMAT, but it was nice to relive the great days and use my brain.

In life we have character building days which are essential to the learning experience. Character building days is a beautiful term that I learned from The Great Les Brown. There are no bad days, please eliminate that term from your vocabulary right now! *Bye Bye Bad Days and Hello Character Building Days*! There is always something to be learnt in a character building day.

This reminds me of that time I had to change a flat tire in the dead of winter. I was speeding to get to work on time at Starbucks; I hit a small pothole that damaged the tire. This was my first car and I have never changed a tire before, I didn't even have the proper tools to change the tire. I found that little nifty thingy (It's called a jack), and placed it under the car but there was no tool to crank it up. I went back into Starbucks and found an old metal syrup pump that I used to crank the jack up. Keep in mind my hands are frozen because I do not like gloves. I was able to get the lug nuts off and replace it with the spare. I could have been upset with the situation and cussed out the world, but I took it as a learning experience. I continued to use the metal syrup pump for other tire changes, I probably should have purchased a brand new car jack!

You have to look for the lessons in negative situations. That character building day taught me how to change a flat tire and becoming disabled at 23 taught me about gratitude. I was always appreciative for my things and accomplishments but I wasn't thankful. I was always concerned with the next goal instead of living in the moment. God has a way of slowing you down so you do not miss something. Did God ever slow you down?

Whatever your purpose is in life use it to make the world a better place. Denzel Washington said it best, "Don't Just Aspire To Make A Living, Aspire To Make A Difference." Give meaning to your life by cherishing the experience and help others to realize their true potential.

Reflect~~ Release ~~Renew

Reflect:

What behaviors come to mind after reading this chapter?

_____

_____

_____

_____

Release:

What behaviors are you going to let go of?

_____

_____

_____

_____

Renew:

How are you going to ensure you are not repeating the behaviors you have released?

_____

_____

_____

_____

Day 3
Are Your Personal Relationships Suffering?

According to the dictionary a "relationship is the way in which two or more concepts, objects, or people are connected, or the state of being connected." These connections are essential to health and wellbeing. Relationships show us how to love and be loved, it also depicts that type of person you want to become.

Poor communication is a clear sign that your personal relationships are suffering. Communication is the cornerstone of a great relationship. Everyone has a unique communicating style; the most common types are passive, aggressive, passive-aggressive, and assertive. The best style to adopt is assertive. Be up front and communicate how you feel to your fellow human. Do not beat around the bush or sweep things under the carpet, because you are afraid of hurting someone's feelings. This will create resentment and anger in the long run.

Let me give you a real life example of resentment and anger from not being up front with my feelings toward my Lady (mother). Lady's greatest accomplishment was regaining custody of all her children to ensure her children became productive members of society. Her accomplishment wasn't good enough for me because I wanted to be in the crowd cheering my mother on, as she did at my high school and college graduations. Lady is extremely intelligent and the world should know of it. With all of her medical knowledge she could have become a pre-eminent individual in the medical world.

Expressing how I felt to Lady could have alleviated a lot of heart-wrenching arguments in my youth and adulthood. Simply express how you feel to your fellow human so you can get a better understanding of their thought process and the why behind a particular decision.

If you are always in an argument, maybe the issue is you! Do you always have to be right? Is it imperative that you have the last word? These are signs that you like to argue. Just because you are invited to an argument doesn't mean you have to participate. That little saying "*Be the bigger person*," can go a long way. It takes two to tango and the same goes for arguments. Try defusing the situation by saying *You're Right* and change the conversation. I promise you it works all the time.

Lack of presence can create a damper in your relationship. It's important to be present in your conversation. If you are texting while conversing you are not present. You must actively listen to the other person. After all you will only retain 10-15 minutes of the conversation, might as well pay attention. Keep an open mind if this conversation is about constructive criticism. Receive what the person is telling you and don't always be so defensive. If the criticism is not helpful, just hit the delete button in your brain.

This reminds me of working for Starbucks and my manager Daniel, used to call me "Swirls and Twirls." At first I was bit offended, but when he explained the reason behind the term I understood what he was trying to teach me. In order to be a great leader you must delegate tasks to your team. Running a business is a team effort and everyone must play a role. If you are the only person running around how can you observe your business and react when a change is needed? This creates ownership and value within the team.

Remember that all relationships have a Reason, a Season, and a Lifetime. DO NOT BE AFRIAD TO LET GO OF TOXIC PEOPLE!! One toxic person that I am letting go of is _____. If you need to add multiple names to that line please do so. A reason usually means a need that you have expressed. They are there to provide you with guidance and support or help you through a difficult time. A season is your turn to share, grow, and learn. They may teach you something you have never done or provide an unbelievable amount of joy. It's real but only for a season. Then you have lifetime relationships that teach you lifetime lessons. Remember to embrace the lessons as they will build a strong foundation to help you deal with life's many ups and downs.

Reflect~~ Release ~~Renew

Reflect:

What behaviors come to mind after reading this chapter?

_____

_____

_____

_____

Release:

What behaviors are you going to let go of?

_____

_____

_____

_____

Renew:

How are you going to ensure you are not repeating the behaviors you have released?

_____

_____

_____

_____

Day 4
Never Feeling Nervous or Scared in Life

If you never feel nervous or scared in life this is a sure sign that you are avoiding risk. Les Brown says it best "You have to Risk to Win." When you take a chance on life, life will take a chance on you Are you taking a chance on life?_____ Now, before you answer that question we must take the lottery out of the equation! Taking a risk in life can be classified as taking a leap into the unknown. This could be starting a business, investing in the stock market, or just going after your dreams. This journey will teach you to have faith. Faith comes from Hearing and Hearing, not by Sight. If you are religious hold tight onto your religious texts and if you believe in the power of energy tune into something positive.

Wayne Dyer said it best, *"When you believe it you will see it."* I had this dream of becoming a speaker and every day I would tell myself you are a speaker. I started to listen to a lot of motivational speakers and I pretended that I was on stage at my 9 to 5 when I spoke to customers. I would pay close attention to my customers' reactions to my wise thoughts and I eliminated those awful filler words (e.g. um, uh, er, ah, like, okay, right, and you know). I decided to attended a Les Brown event in New Jersey on November 19, 2017. Pay close attention to how powerful the universe is. *I sat in the first row. I was able to speak with Les Brown and take a picture with him. I gave him my business card and a few members of his staff. I was invited to a free dinner in Florida in April 2018, provided that I attend a speakers training.* This training jumped started my speaking career and I later found out that dinner was $500 a plate. The faster you run toward your dreams, the faster your dreams run toward you.

Remember to Embrace the Butterflies. Life is like a series of first dates; You put on the best outfit, You hope s/he smells good, Will s/he like me?, Will there be a second date? Your nervousness will trigger your flight or fight response. Are you going to give into your fears or duke it out? Flight gives you the option to run and fight ensures your focus on the task at hand. When you make the decision to succeed the world falls to the background and you're empowered to do any and everything!

It's all a matter of practice. You can train yourself to become a good fighter. You can ensure that you come out swinging instead of running. You do this by believing in yourself and conditioning the mind. Look in that mirror and tell yourself "I Can and I am," to whatever it is that you want to achieve. You will then start to believe. Condition your mind with positive words or thoughts of encouragement. If you are going on an interview for a new job you have to have the mindset that it is already yours. It doesn't matter how many applicants apply for the position, it is yours!

You must get out of your comfort zone to succeed in this new era of life. It is no longer about surviving; you must separate yourself from the masses. What's unique about you that Tom, Sue, or Johnny the robot doesn't have? We are in the era of The Entrepreneur and the 40/40/40 plan is no more. The 40/40/40 plan simply states you work on a job for 40 hours a week, retire after 40 years, and live off of 40% of your income. If you do not want to struggle in your senior years, I suggest creating a new plan.

Sales is a great way to get out of your comfort zone. If you do not take sales seriously you are telling the universe you do not want cash. If you do not love cash, please close this book right now! I learned that I was a sales person when I entered the world of network marketing. I started my own coffee business with Organo Gold. Coffee made sense because I was a manager at Starbucks for almost 6 years, I knew how much people loved coffee. The beauty of Organo Gold's products was an ancient herb called ganoderma. It infused medicinal properties into the coffee. Networking marketing is not for everyone; you can also start a micro-business. Micro-businesses can be ran by one or two people and it has low overhead costs. Some of my micro-businesses were selling cakes and pies, bagging bags in the supermarket (I did this in my youth), and doing hair. What type of micro-business can you start?_____

Risk is a key element to success and failure is the only way to succeed. Failure tells you that you are on your way. There's a product called WD-40 which stands for "Water Displacement 40th Attempt." We use it to quiet squeaky door hinges. It took the scientists 39 times before they perfected it. On the 40th time it was perfected. Never give up and embrace your failures.

Reflect~~ Release ~~Renew

Reflect:

What behaviors come to mind after reading this chapter?

_____

_____

_____

_____

Release:

What behaviors are you going to let go of?

_____

_____

_____

_____

Renew:

How are you going to ensure you are not repeating the behaviors you have released?

_____

_____

_____

_____

Day 5
Fear of Change

      Fear of change is one of the most common fears that people face. People resist change because they believe they will lose something of value or control. What type of change have you feared?_____

Everything seems different and it causes people to be paralyzed in situations that are not healthy or fulfilling. As difficult as it sounds try to embrace change, there's always a valuable lesson in every experience. Master the lesson and move forward in your journey.

There are 3 types of fear and 4 stages of fear. The 3 types of fear are; Fear of the unknown, Fear of failure, and Fear of success. In order for you to better understand the stages of fear, let's imagine you are moving to a new home.

Stage 1 is Anticipation. This is the excitement stage. Think about all of the benefits of a new home; the new smell, you can decorate, new furniture, or the overall feeling of having something new.

Stage 2 is Regression. This is when things get worse before it gets better. You might uncover the house has structural problems or termites.

Stage 3 is Breakthrough. This is when you finally see the light at the end of the tunnel. You figure out how to solve the problems you have uncovered. You find an experienced structural engineer to address the foundation issue and an exterminator to help with the termites.

Stage 4 is Consolidation. Returning to your scheduled programming. You are experiencing the new norm, everything is how you originally imagined.

Fear of change limits you and holds you back from Greatness. It's okay to "*take a leap of faith and grow wings on the way down*," Thank You Les Brown. He has these wise sayings and I just love to quote. What can you take a leap of faith on?

I remember when I decided I was going to become a travel YouTuber. I had no idea as to what or how I was going to accomplish my mission, but I did what any good millennial would do. I went to YouTube and typed in "How do you start a YouTube Channel?" Everything that I needed to start a YouTube channel was already on YouTube, all I had to do was follow the example. I learned how to create a banner for my channel, organize my channel with playlists, and how to edit and rank my videos. Refrain from wanting it to be perfect, getting started counts most.

If you are implementing change remember to be compassionate and put yourself in the other person's shoes. Everyone reacts differently to change and you should not categorize people. Be the example of change that you are trying to implement. Plan your change and take everyone's concerns in to consideration, whether it's personal relationships or in an organization. Now, I bet you're thinking what if someone turns against you? This is likely to happen and I want you to remember 3 key phrases; Agree, Agree, and Always Agree. This will ensure that you are on their side and that you completely understand their needs (e.g. It is unfair that I have to change my schedule and the other employees do not. Tom you are absolutely right it is unfair that you have to change your schedule. However, you are most qualified for this task and I know I can depend on you). Give a little candy with the medicine and they will eat it up.

In order for change to stick you have to Expect the best, Prepare for the worst, and Capitalize on what comes. Make up your mind that everything is happing for the greater good. There is no such thing as bad luck you are right where you're supposed to be. Whatever the change is look on the bright side and know that it will work out in your favor. This reminds me of working in retail and I had 4 different district managers in 6 months. As a manager this might seem overwhelming because you have to prove your leadership skills each time. My approach was a bit unconventional, I allowed my work ethic to speak for itself and for my district manager to adjust to me. If we bleed the same then we are the same kind of people. Your title does not scare me, if you are always ready you do not have to get ready! This approach made me stand out from my peers.

Reflect~~ Release ~~Renew

Reflect:

What behaviors come to mind after reading this chapter?

_____

_____

_____

_____

Release:

What behaviors are you going to let go of?

_____

_____

_____

_____

Renew:

How are you going to ensure you are not repeating the behaviors you have released?

_____

_____

_____

_____

Day 6
Taking Steps to Improve Yourself

    We can all improve on something; nobody in this world is perfect. Before I dive into what I feel people can improve on, I want you to dig deep within yourself and see what you can improve on. I can improve on _____ , _____ , _____ . The idea of improving self means that you are aware that you can be so much more than what you already are!
The most important thing about improving yourself is self-image. When you look in the mirror what do you see? When I look in the mirror I see a beautiful chocolate man who is wonderfully made. If you cannot describe yourself as eloquently as I just did about me, we have some work to do! You are the best thing since sliced bread. I want you to get in the mirror and appreciate what you see. Tell yourself how beautiful you are and what you love most about you. Let's take it a step further, take a selfie of yourself and look at it three times a day. Just as if you were looking at yourself in the mirror, say the same exact *"sweet nothings"* (as I like to call it).

Spend time getting to know self! Take yourself on a date or eat your favorite snack. It's okay to take yourself out on a nice date; I promise you are not crazy! You are telling the universe how you desire to be treated and you will attract a person to treat you the same way. Ask yourself how are you doing today? Do you feel happy? Do you feel tired? Address the questions you are asking self; if you do not feel happy do the things that make you happy. If you feel tired it's time to get some more rest.

Getting to know self will make you self-aware of your thoughts and what's going on in that big noodle. It's best to journal your thoughts so you can easily process your feelings. I have a list called Light Bulb. I write down all of my genius ideas. Experts estimate we have 60,000 to 80,000 thoughts a day. Suppose 10% of those thoughts are million dollar ideas? Do not let your gold mine slip away. Learn to admit to your mistakes and control your ego. EGO can stand for edging god out. We are edging god out by being blind to the realties that we are creating. If you are not a god lover, you are creating energy that you do not want in your life!

Remember, it's okay to say no to the things that do not serve you. You can tie it all together with mediation. Meditating will help you center the mind, heal the body, and get rid of those icky thoughts.

Avoid the negativity, whether it's people or a bad habit. That old saying misery loves company is very true. Negative people are like the common cold, easy to get and a process to get rid of. Protect your thoughts and feed them with a long handle spoon. Suppose there's a person in your life that you cannot easily let go of, zero in on what you like most about that person and delete the garbage that doesn't serve you. Most times this is usually a co-worker or a family member. The same goes for bad habits; let go of them. What are three negative habits that do not serve you? _____, _____, _____.
Through all of the negativity remember to laugh laugh laugh! It's the best way to get through a difficult situation. Did you know 1 minute of laughter will boost the immune system for 24hrs? Laughter is the best medicine for healing. Spend your time with people that have a great aura and love to laugh.

An attitude of gratitude will increase your overall happiness and bring more into your life. When you take notice and reflect upon the little things and past experiences; you will decrease stress, depression, and anxiety. I give thanks every time I take public transportation. I remember when my agoraphobia would not allow me to get on a train, bus, or a plane. Appreciating what you have and rejecting consumerism is a part of gratitude. Do you really need every new pair of Jordan's that comes to the market? You would benefit more if you owned a piece of the company. Learn to serve people; serving is the rent you pay to be on earth. It's okay to do more than your pay grade. Help people for the sake of helping others, the joy that is expressed is the best payment. You will feel on top of the world.

Lastly, find a mentor if you want to completely elevate yourself.
Jim Rohn says it best, "Don't wish it was easier, wish you were better." Find a mentor that can teach you the tips and tricks of your trade. My mentor, Antonio T. Smith Jr. is helping me to elevate my brand and become a millionaire. I am learning the ins and outs of business, social media marketing, and the speaking industry. Emulation is highest form of

flattery. Follow what they are doing and add your own flavor. If all else fails pick up a book. You can learn so much if you read daily.

Reflect~~ Release ~~Renew

Reflect:

What behaviors come to mind after reading this chapter?

_____

_____

_____

_____

Release:

What behaviors are you going to let go of?

_____

_____

_____

_____

Renew:

How are you going to ensure you are not repeating the behaviors you have released?

_____

_____

_____

_____

Day 7
Are You Coasting in Life?

According to the dictionary the meaning of coasting is *moving easily without using power.* When you add life to the equation you are doing the bare minimum to get by. You know you are capable of doing so much more but you decide not to put the effort in. If you are doing the bare minimum please do not expect advancement or new opportunities to head your way. The energy that you put into the universe will come back to you tenfold. I challenge you to ask yourself are you coasting in life?

___

Where do you see yourself in a year?
___

___

If you are just punching the clock you are coasting in life! Margret's shift starts at 8am, but she arrives 8ish. It's not her fault that she's late; the train had delays, little JoJo forgot his homework at home and she had to turn back to retrieve it, the list can go on. Margret should just take responsibility for her actions and plan accordingly; maybe she should take an earlier train and ensure that JoJo's bag is packed the night before. Margret continues to complain about her life the entire shift and avoids doing work at any cost. It just grinds my gears (I hope you caught this Family Guy reference) to hear people complain about their job or their lives at the work place. I make it a point to ask that individual why do you work here if this job is so terrible? Please take your negative energy somewhere else. If you have a bit of Margret within you, I need you to check your heart space.

It's time to lose the mentality "This is not in my job description." It's okay to serve others or go above and beyond without expecting something in return. Serving others is the rent we pay to be on earth. This reminds me of working as a manager in Starbucks, I would always tell my employees we are in the trenches together. I would never ask my employees to do something that I personally would never do. Everyone's least favorite task at Starbucks is cleaning the customer restroom because it's always in disarray. Cleaning the restroom is not in a manager's description; however I would always clean it to show my employees that we are one team. If I do it, I expect for you to do it as well!

Procrastination is your ugly best friend with bad make up. For my fellas, that's your dawg with no game and the worst wing man. The easiest way to avoid procrastination is to set up a daily 3 Step list. Little steps equal one giant step. Be sure to outline your 3 step list for a week or month. This will ensure that you are always productive and you are getting things done. We are all human and life does get in the way, if you did not complete one of your steps please add it to the next day and make sure it's at the top of the list. Do not become one of those individuals that are always adding things to the list. Hold yourself accountable and get it done. If you have to cut out the television or a get together to complete your steps, please do so! Your goals will become clear and you can easily measure your success.

When you enter the workplace consider your mindset. The workplace can be your business or a company that you work for. Ask yourself who are you becoming? Are you happy? Do you feel successful? Are you excited? If you have negative responses to any of these questions it's time to plan your exit. You do not have to stay anywhere that does not serve you. The secret to life is to be HaPpY and you must do things that make you HaPpY! It made me HaPpY to type HaPpY this way, I hope it made you chuckle. Did you know most people have a heart attack on Monday morning between the hours of 7-10am? Do not be one of those people that dreads Sunday nights and Monday morning because it's back to that boring, unhappy, no good job. Be excited about life so you are not just coasting.

What is the secret to Life?
___

How do you be Happy?
___

Reflect~~ Release ~~Renew

Reflect:

What behaviors come to mind after reading this chapter?

_____

_____

_____

Release:

What behaviors are you going to let go of?

_____

_____

_____

_____

Renew:

How are you going to ensure you are not repeating the behaviors you have released?

_____

_____

_____

_____

Day 8
Taking Life and Its Gifts for Granted

Taking Life and its Gifts for Granted means to not appreciate or realize how much something really means to you. Life is so precious and you must cherish it every step of the way. Your talents are gifts that are granted to you. If you do not appreciate or use your gifts they will be taken away. What are some of your gifts?

_____

It's imperative that you are thankful for the little things; your loved ones, daily meals, and clothes on your back. Growing up in foster care I didn't always have a hot meal or clean clothes to wear. I make sure I do not waste food and when I buy a new article of clothing I always give something away. In 2016, I traveled to Cambodia and visited a Cambodian village where I noticed children with no beds. I couldn't fathom children sleeping on the bare floor and still being happy go lucky. This experience reminded me to be thankful for the bed that I sleep in every single night. If you want to grow as a human I implore you to travel and see how other people live around the world. Something as simple as toilet tissue in a public restroom is considered a luxury in another country.

Life is short! Stop putting things off. If you want to do something make a plan and get it done. My plan was to travel the world after I graduated college and I became disabled with agoraphobia and panic disorder. It took five long years before I was able to get on a plane. Now, that I am able to manage my agoraphobia I have been to ten countries on two different continents. Nothing lasts forever you must appreciate where you are and what you have. Agoraphobia taught me not to put things off; life will take away what you fail to appreciate.

If you do not use your gifts God will take them back. Figure out your passion and purpose and use your gifts to maximize it. Passion is the emotion or why behind your purpose. Your purpose is what you feel you're destined to do or be on earth. What are you destined to do or be on earth?

_____

_____

Not using your gifts signals the universe that you are lacking gratitude. One of my gifts is speaking and it has allowed me to become a transformational entertainer. I have a way with words and how I utilize body language.

Are you counting your misfortunes? Do not cast your blessings to the wayside. Just because your house burnt down, doesn't mean life is over. Are you still breathing? Is your family okay? Things can always be replaced; however you cannot replace a life. It's hard when a loved one passes away, but you can't let it break you. It's best to focus on the memories that you made and that person will always be in your heart. The bright side is that you have a guardian angel looking over you. Do not count your misfortunes, embrace the lessons and always look to the bright side. There's a lesson in every experience.

Noticing your surroundings is the most important part about this chapter. It's time to get off those screens. Social media has the world wrapped up in other people's lives and losing sight of what's most important. Your life is just as fabulous as the celebrities on your screen. The work we do, the people we love, and the things we experience are most important. These experiences can be good or bad because there is a lesson in every experience. Pay attention to the sunshine, the birds chirping, and the cleansing of the rain. Remember it's okay to help others. Find an organization to give back to or help family and friends. It's okay to lend help to stranger; i.e. holding a door, carrying a stroller down the stairs, or helping the elderly with a bag. Be mindful of your surroundings and help out any way possible.

Reflect~~ Release ~~Renew

Reflect:

What behaviors come to mind after reading this chapter?

_____

_____

_____

_____

Release:

What behaviors are you going to let go of?

_____

_____

_____

_____

Renew:

How are you going to ensure you are not repeating the behaviors you have released?

_____

_____

_____

_____

Day 9
Are You a Doormat?

The definition of a doormat is a person that bends over backwards to please people. This term is mostly associated with women and men who are considered weak or wimps. However, I believe men and woman can both be described as doormats. There are five clear signs that you are suffering from doormat syndrome (This is not a scientific discovery, just a lovely term that I came up with.)

First Sign- Always apologetic (You are always apologizing for silly mistakes)

Second Sign- Playing the victim (Woe is me, everything always happens to you)

Third Sign- Expect to be treated poorly (You expect for people to use and abuse you)

Fourth Sign- Needs constant approval (Before you act you must receive approval from another human)

Fifth Sign- Always complaining (You're always complaining to others about the injustice in your world)

If you show signs of all five you have a lot of work ahead of yourself! If you show one or two signs it will be a simple adjustment and a check of your heart space. Your heart space is your emotions, sometimes we have to take self out of the equation. I had an employee that was suffering from Doormat Syndrome and her greatest down fall was seeking approval from others. If she didn't receive my approval on her work she could not move forward and her world would fall apart. To rectify the situation I would intentionally not give her approval and force her to become her own individual.

Do you use the term "It's Just Life?" _____. No it's not just life, it's you. What you think about you bring about. The company you keep you will reap. You are the deciding factor on how people treat you and the thoughts that run through your head. How you feel on the inside is what you will attract to you. When I walk you know I am the Sh*t. Confidence exudes from skin like an enchanting spell. If you do not believe you are the best thing walking, nobody else will. Make sure your needs are being met. One common misconception that I come across is that the child's needs come before a parent. As a parent you must take care of yourself before you can provide for someone else. When you are on an airplane the flight attendant always instructs you to put on your oxygen mask before you assist someone else. How can you help someone with their oxygen mask if you are gasping for air? When it comes to your needs you matter!

Do you hope someone will acknowledge your acts of kindness? _____. You stay late at work and no one noticed, you buy people's affection while resenting them, and you are looking for something in return for your kindness. If you are doing something out the goodness of your heart you should never expect something in return. If you feel as though you are being taking advantage of, it's okay to say no or limit your acts of kindness. Please do not confuse your rejected acts of kindness with someone disliking the nice guy. We all love to receive nice things and acts of kindness. The hard truth is that no one likes a spineless individual pandering for their affection. Tossing yourself at someone's feet with no self-worth will never make you feel on top of the world. Self-confidence equal's attractiveness, striving to prove yourself equal's unattractiveness.

Are you living for a relationship? _____. If your life revolves around your significant other you are borderline doormat. This will lead you to falling victim of one of the five signs. It's okay to have hobbies or other friends outside of your relationship. It's important to not lose sight of yourself or feel as though you need your partner to complete you. Let's say the relationship doesn't work and you start to question yourself. Am I the reason why they dumped me? Am I too nice? Did I lack in attention? There is nothing wrong with you, both parties had their issues. Reflect on the type of relationship you want and continue to express how you feel. Never let anything fester in a relationship, it will always come back to bite you in the tail.

Reflect~~ Release ~~Renew

Reflect:

What behaviors come to mind after reading this chapter?

_____

_____

_____

_____

Release:

What behaviors are you going to let go of?

_____

_____

_____

_____

Renew:

How are you going to ensure you are not repeating the behaviors you have released?

_____

_____

_____

_____

Day 10
Financial Complacency

Financial Complacency is not a strategy, it's a death sentence. If you have more month than money at the end of every pay cycle, you need a new strategy! Financial complacency is usually the result of consumerism. Consumerism is a social and economic order that encourages the purchase of goods and services in ever-greater amounts. In other words do not buy more than what is needed, although you see a sign called "*Sale.*" It's not a sale it's a ploy to get you to spend more. If you can't purchase it 7 times over, you are not meant to have it at that time. Consider buying that new car at a later date. What product/service are you considering purchasing that you cannot purchase 7 times over?

It's best to live by Zero Balance, a term that I learned from Dr. Shirley Davis. Make sure you account for every dollar spent. It doesn't matter how much money you make, it matters how much is left over. Are your left over dollars creating new babies to make you more money? Money is a vehicle that works for you. You should never be working for it. If you make 300K per year and you spend 400K, sorry you're in debt. This is still considered living pay check to pay check; all you did was increase your pay grade. A rise in income is not permission to spend more. Create a plan where your money can make you more money (#investing) or pay off debt.

Be sure to include yourself in your monthly expenses. Yes, that's right you are the first bill that you pay. If you have to physically create a bill with your name on it to ensure that you pay you, please do so! You cannot have the riches of the world if you do not pay yourself first. Ten percent of your income should go toward investing in a greater future. Notice how I didn't say 'Retirement.' I associate retirement with death; the only time you should retire from something is if it no longer serves you. That greater future is doing whatever makes you happy! I am currently living by the twenty percent rule; 10% goes to investing, 10% to Law's Adventures, and I live off of 80%. My mission is to live off of 70% of my income, invest 30%, and have my assets pay for Law's Adventures. In order to pull this off I need multiple streams of income, I currently have 18 on my list!

How many streams of income are you working on or already have in play?

_____

_____

I bet you are asking How Do You Budget? Well, there's no right or wrong way to budget; you have to figure out what works best for your situation. The most important factor is that you keep your expenses low. I manage my expenses by putting everything on one credit card and once I reach my monthly allotment no more spending. This allows me to accurately track where my money is going. Suppose that establishment does not take credit cards? Well, I always keep an emergency $20 dollar bill. I do not spend my liquid (cash in the bank) because it's for making me more babies! Depending on the type of credit card that you have never spend more than 30% of your credit card limit. In my case I do not have one; I haven't since the age of 20. I guess I am doing something right! I don't believe in paying the minimum payment per month, that's a way for the credit institutions to make money off of you (i.e. interest rates and late payment fees). Never spend more than what you have. Create your budget and stick to it! Start to ponder what you want to have financially. It's always good having an idea of what you want for your life. Check out my personal financial goals and use it as a guide to create your own plan.

My Financial Plan

30 Day Goal

$25,000

6 Month Goal

$100, 000

1 Year

$2 Million a Year minimum to make Year over Year (Of course it will increase)

3 Years

$6 Million Liquid saved

10 Year

$50 Million Liquid saved

Greater Years (Tender Young age of 80-100)

$1 Billion Saved

I implore you to let go of those misplaced priorities. I have a list of questions that I want you ponder and decide on. ***Do you have to wear labels?*** *"Clothes don't maketh man, man maketh clothes."* Nobody cares what you are wearing, what matters is what comes out of your mouth. Foster care taught me how to dress with few options and nobody caught on. ***Do you have to drive the most expensive car?*** If you cannot buy it 7 times over it is not meant for you at this time. Consider getting something more affordable if you truly need a car to get you from A to B. ***Do you just buy or do you compare prices?*** Nothing wrong with considering cost when you are purchasing products and services. You want the bang for your buck. Spend your money wisely because anyone can be one funeral or surgery away from being broke. ***Have you checked your credit report lately?*** It's important to know what the credit bureau is saying about you! Your credit score is a report of your integrity. Be sure to clear up any abnormalities, you have a right to fight any derogatory marks.

If you take anything away from Day 10 know that your millionaire and billionaire status is based on how much money you keep not how much you make!

Reflect~~ Release ~~Renew

Reflect:

What behaviors come to mind after reading this chapter?

_____

_____

_____

_____

Release:

What behaviors are you going to let go of?

_____

_____

_____

_____

Renew:

How are you going to ensure you are not repeating the behaviors you have released?

_____

_____

_____

_____

_____

Day 11
Physical Complacency

      Physical complacency can spread like wild fire and often leads to some of the worst outcomes that we regret. Many people may not know they are settling until the pains and aches of life start to creep in. The most common signs are disease, mental health challenges, and joint issues. I do not believe in that three letter word **OLD.** You are as young as you feel; if you are 80 years old, you are 80 years young. How many years young are you? _____ young. It's a different kind of young, a type of young that you navigate with your mind. Make it up in your mind how young you are and always remain a kid at heart. Your joy is what pushes you forward in life, find the little silly things that make you laugh. Your mind allows you to create your reality. I am going to live until 100 and God will take the wheel after that. I was born in 1988 and I must see 2088. The number 8 is embedded in my soul. Shall I remind you of what eight means? Eight mean prosperity in the Asian cultures and new beginnings in the book of life. I have 8 letters in my first, middle, and last name. I am one of 8, I was born in '88, I am the third child, 3+5= 8. Did I mention 8 is my favorite number?

It's important to be conscious of what you are placing inside of your temple. Your body is your temple and you must respect it as a sacred work of art. What type of eating habits do you practice? How do you feel after you have eaten a meal? After you finish eating you should be energized and ready to tackle any task. If you feel sluggish or in need of a nap, it's time to rethink your eating habits. A plant based diet is the best routine to living a Great Life. There are lots of studies online that would agree, check out the document 'What the Health on Netflix.' I practice a vegan life style; no meat, no seafood, no dairy, and no eggs. I love how my body feels and the energy level. I love that I am hardly ever sick. If I do get sick it's a clear sign that I ate something that I wasn't supposed to or the product had some type of animal fat. Vegan life isn't for everyone so listen to your body! The same goes for what you eat, pay close attention to how your body reacts to the food that you eat. If you feel terrible after you eat something, please do yourself a favor and stop eating it.

If you want to ensure your longevity on this earth you absolutely need a work out regimen. In the words of my Yoga Mentor Fleurette, "You got to keep those areas JUICY." How often do you work out? _____. If it's less than 2 times a week you have some serious changes to commit to. Working out helps to release endorphins, you know those happy hormones. They help to release pain and keep you in a state of euphoria. When I decided to kick my panic disorder medications the gym became my new drug. The gym kept me happy and full of life. I've released weight on two occasions, at 16 years old and 25 years old. Age 16, I went from a size 42 to a 33. Age 25, I went from a size 40 to 31. Please let the record show there will not be a third time! Now, don't be so quick to join a gym. Most people join a gym and never go, double back to Day 10 Financial Complacency: Where is your money going to? Fast walking, jogging, and calisthenics are just as effective as joining a gym. Since, you are working on your body you might as well work on your mind. You can exercise your brain by reading, taking a new class, or puzzles that challenge the brain like Sudoku.

Make sure you get an adequate amount of rest each night. Sleep requirements can vary from person to person; the standard amount of rest is 7 to 9 hours. Listen to your body. It will tell you if you are not getting enough rest at night. During deep sleep your body works to repair muscle, organs, and other cells. Chemicals that strengthen your immune system start to circulate in your blood. Without adequate sleep, you can get behind in your healing, and problems build up. Make sure you have a consistent bed time routine and avoid light. Turn off your phone and TV as they distract you from falling into a deep sleep. If you are experiencing energy crashes during the day that is a sign of lack of sleep and/or diet issues. Sleep is important for my health because I dealt with delirium. I went a week without sleep and I fell into a deep psychosis. Psychosis is a loss of reality, you do not know if you're coming or going. We will save this story for another book (#IODH).

Mental health is extremely important to releasing physical complacency. You must monitor your thoughts and check your heart space. How are you feeling on the inside? If you feel something is wrong do not be afraid to seek help. Depression is the second leading medical cause of disability in the USA.

There are six signs of depression:

1. Sad, empty, helplessness, worthlessness
2. Irritability
3. Less interested in activities (less meaning you love an activity, but now it feels too tiresome to do it)
4. Changes in your sleep patterns
5. Loss of Appetite
6. Aches and Pains

If you are experiencing any of these changes, I would seek counseling to be certain you are not experiencing depression. Some of the major triggers of depression are life events, substance abuse, and trauma (Childhood and/or Adulthood). Signs of depression and triggers can affect each person differently. I am by no means a medical professional. I am speaking from past experiences. If you identify with any of what I said, please seek medical help. There is nothing wrong getting a second opinion to make sure you keep your beauty intact. **YOU ARE BEAUTIFUL AND WONDERFULLY MADE!**

Reflect~~ Release ~~Renew

Reflect:

What behaviors come to mind after reading this chapter?

_____

_____

_____

_____

Release:

What behaviors are you going to let go of?

_____

_____

_____

_____

Renew:

How are you going to ensure you are not repeating the behaviors you have released?

_____

_____

_____

_____

_____

Day 12
Forgiveness

According to a psychologist the act of forgiveness is a conscious, deliberate decision to release feelings of resentment or vengeance toward a person or group who has harmed you, regardless of whether they actually deserve your forgiveness.

In order to forgive you must know what it is not:

1. Forgiveness doesn't mean you are pardoning the other person's actions
2. Forgiveness doesn't mean you need to tell the person that s/he is forgiven
3. Forgiveness doesn't mean you shouldn't have any more feelings about the situation
4. Forgiveness doesn't mean there is nothing further to work out in the relationship or everything is okay
5. Forgiveness doesn't mean you should forget the incident ever happened
6. Forgiveness doesn't mean you have to continue to include the person in your life
7. Forgiveness isn't something you do for the other person
8. **FORGIVENESS IS FOR YOU!**

When you forgive you are accepting the reality of what happened. You find a way to live in a state of resolution. This can be a gradual process and doesn't have to include that person. It's not about the person who wronged you, it's for You! This process will allow you to heal and make peace with the reality of what happened to you. It was a process to forgive my parents for their mistakes that resulted in my upbringing in foster care.

My mother didn't always have the easiest time trying to finish raising her children. You have to undo what a child is already accustomed to. On top of all that the feeling of abandonment isn't something that easily goes away. It seeps into your relationships like grass stains on a white cotton shirt. It's very easy for me to dismiss people before they have a chance to walk out of my life. Forgiveness has allowed me to work with my abandonment issues and build fulfilling relationships. What person or persons do you need to forgive?

_____

_____

Why is forgiveness so hard? You're filled with thoughts of retribution or revenge. You might feel as though you have a moral right to get even, or maybe you just plain ol' want to get even, and it doesn't matter who. You think the act of getting even will make you feel superior to the person or persons that wronged you. Kimberly Elise's character *Helen* in *Tyler Perry's Diary of a Mad Black Woman*, thought she would feel superior if she abused her disabled husband because of how he treated her. The revenge felt sweet in the beginning and she won her husband back. It didn't change anything because she didn't forgive her husband. She began to feel sad and longed for the love of the second man who treated her right. Forgiveness is the sweetest retribution you can ever have. It releases all ill feelings and you can move on with life. There is no wrong or right way to forgive. You have to decide what is best for you. You can confront the person or write it in a letter. I chose to write a letter to my eldest brother on how he made me feel growing up gay. He said he knew I meant business because it was in words. The written language can be the best form of expression. You can choose to give your letter to the person or burn it. Either way just get those feelings out of you.

You must ask yourself do you want to forgive or are you addicted to the anger? Anger can taste as sweet as candy, which is why so many people have a hard time with letting it go. Don't allow anger to make you mad at the world or allow someone else to pay for the mistakes of the wronged. You are not a victim, you are a victor. It requires will power to forgive another human. It's hard because the hurt cuts so deep; that person was too abusive, that person expressed no regret, you must identify your pain before you forgive. There are four steps to forgive and mini questions to consider when you are forgiving.

4 Steps to Forgive:

1. Accept the incident that occurred
    a. Accept how you felt
    b. How it made you react
    c. Acknowledge the reality of what occurred
2. Acknowledge the growth you experienced as a result of the incident
    a. What did you learn about yourself?
    b. Think about your needs and boundaries
    c. Remember you survived from the incident and grew from it
3. Think of the other person
    a. We are all flawed as human beings
    b. He or she acted from limited beliefs and a skewed frame of reference
    c. Your hurt was a need the person was to trying to fulfill
4. Decide whether or not you want to tell that person you forgive them
    a. Decide on the best method to forgive the person
    b. In person or a letter
    c. Use the words "I forgive you"
    d. Give an explanation of your forgiveness

If you decide not to forgive prepare yourself for a world of anger and bitterness. You will be unhappy, picking a fight for every little thing. Every time you see that individual their presence will bother you and you will avoid talking to them. Wishing ill will on someone else will come back to you. Karma always repeats itself and you will give that person power over you. Do yourself a favor and forgive.

FORGIVENESS IS LOVING WITHOUT ANGER!!

Reflect~~ Release ~~Renew

Reflect:

What behaviors come to mind after reading this chapter?

___

Release:

What behaviors are you going to let go of?

___

Renew:

How are you going to ensure you are not repeating the behaviors you have released?

___

Day 13
Forgiveness Part II

      Lack of forgiveness will lead a human down the wrong path. It will cause you to feel as though the world owes you something and you make others pay for the mistakes of the wronged. I am going use my relationship with my father, formerly known as sperm donor. Yes, that's right I would often refer to my father as sperm donor. He didn't deserve the title father or dad because he walked out of my life too many times. You might think I am crazy for forgiving him on so many occasions. It's important to always be in a state of forgiveness. I learned from Antonio T. Smith Jr. to forgive a person in advance. There will always be someone to wrong you. Try not to hold on to ill feelings!

Your dad is supposed to be your superhero, the one who rids the world of monsters and can solve any problem. I once felt this way about my father and other times he was just the man who created me. Oddly enough I am a splitting image of him. Imagined every time you look in the mirror you saw your father. At the age of 17 my father got severely sick and needed help with everything. I remember being in that hospital and his father did not recognize me. I guess jacka** is hereditary, mind you I am a splitting image of my father. My father needed help to the restroom and the nurse looked in the direction of his father. His reply, "I am not helping no grown a** man wipe his a**." No wonder my father was an idiot; he had a great example. Of course, I assisted my father in the restroom.

Before we dive deeper, keep in mind that my father is part of the reason why I was placed into foster care on two separate occasions. If you forgot go back to Day 1. Fast forward to my college graduation, my father and I had a silly argument about taxes and he didn't come to my college graduation. I informed my father to forgo claiming my younger sister on his taxes because she already filed. He took it as if I was getting into his financial business. Black folk can be a little sensitive when it comes to money and a child is supposed to always stay in a child's place, regardless of age. A few choice words were exchanged and my father allowed his pride to get the best of him. I was his first child to graduate college and he decided not to come. It didn't matter what the argument was about he should have been there.

The next time I spoke to my father I was severely sick in the hospital at the age of 23. For those of you who are not a mathematician, I graduated college at 21 and was sick two years later. I bet you are thinking my father took care of me like I took care of him at 17 years old. Yeah, right (Insert laughter)! My father acted like a pure fool. My mother invited him because I wasn't doing so well. My father entered the hospital room with a gift and his girlfriend Diane. She greeted me and I just looked at him. Diane gave us some time to ourselves to hash things out. That was the worst thing Diane could have ever done. Please cue the dramatic music...

Law: "I do not have anything to say to you."
Father: "I only came on the account of your mother."
Law: "Since you only came on the account of my mother and both of you created me There's The DOOR!"
Father: Storms out. Dragging his gift behind him. The balloons would not leave so he had to pull twice (insert laughter).
Diane: "What happened Lawrence?"
Law: "My father will always be my father!"
Father: Yells in the room, "Come on before I leave you."
Law: "I am used to this. Don't miss your ride."
Diane: "I love you Lawrence."

My father and I were estranged for six years before I heard from him again. He never checked on me to see if I made it out of the hospital. He didn't know I became disabled at 23 and wouldn't leave the house for two years. One day out of the blue, he called and left a voicemail wanting to apologize for all his wrong doing. I listened to that voicemail a couple of times and I waited a week for before I responded. You know for dramatic affect. In the voicemail he stated "I probably hate him and he understands if I do not reach out." I thought to myself wooow, this man really doesn't know his son. Why would I waste energy hating someone? When I responded to him via text, I made sure to explain that I would never waste energy hating someone and that I would only speak to him face to face.

My father and I were able to move past our issues. I am able to refer to him as father, still working on calling him father or dad. He has to earn that title. He's in a position where he really needs my help. He deals with COPD and must be on oxygen 18 hours a day. That summer we hashed things out, I spent a month running back and forth to the hospital, for a man that walked in and out of my life. That journey helped to give birth to this book. Forgiving him gave me permission to be there for him. Imagine bathing or cooking for a person that you have not forgiven. You probably would want to commit bodily harm to them. One of the most important things I told my father is that all we have in this life is our name and our memories. Let's make memories!

Just in case you were wondering my father's name is David. What's your father's name?

Reflect~~ Release ~~Renew

Reflect:

What behaviors come to mind after reading this chapter?

_____

_____

_____

_____

Release:

What behaviors are you going to let go of?

_____

_____

_____

Renew:

How are you going to ensure you are not repeating the behaviors you have released?

_____

_____

_____

_____

_____

12 Ways to Master Your Choice

Day 14
Set Up New Goals

Congratulations on moving past the 12 Pitfalls of not Mastering Your Choice. You are well on your way in releasing complacency from your life. You read my story on how I could have been complacent and the 12 Pitfalls of Complacency.
Feel free to re-read any of the 12 Pitfalls:

1. Do You See Life As A Learning Experience?
2. Are Your Personal Relationships Suffering?
3. Never Feeling Nervous or Scared in Life.
4. Fear of Change.
5. Taking Steps to Improve Yourself.
6. Are you Coasting in Life?
7. Taking Life and It's Gifts for Granted.
8. Are You a Doormat?
9. Financial Complacency.
10. Physical Complacency.
11. Forgiveness.
12. Forgiveness Part II.

Zig Ziglar said it best, "A goal properly set is halfway reached." Without goals you lack focus and direction. Goals allow you to take control of your life's direction and it provides a benchmark for determining whether you are actually succeeding. There are five golden rules you must consider before you establish a goal.

Five Golden Rules

1. Set Goals That Motivate You
2. Set SMART GOALS
3. Set Goals in Writing
4. Make an Action Plan
5. Stick with it

Make sure you set goals that motivate you. Your goals must be important and consider the value in achieving them. Do you give high priority to the goals in your life? _____. If you are not laser focused, you will give yourself too many goals to consider and eventually just give up. What is your reason for setting this goal? If your why doesn't make your cry you must find a new reason to push you forward. The importance of having a strong why is so you have something to fall back on when times get hard. Your why will give you a sense of urgency and ensure a must do attitude to accomplish your goals. You can be and do whatever you put your mind to. Remember this simple equation: thoughts + emotions= creation. If you see it in your mind you can hold it in your hand.

Live by S.M.A.R.T goals; SMART stands for **S**pecific, **M**easurable, **A**ttainable, **R**elevant, and **T**ime. To better explain **SMART** we are going to use my goal of becoming a professional speaker. **S:** I want to become an International Speaker. **M:** Time to manifest what I want. I take time out of my day to visualize myself on stage. I can hear the crowd cheering me on and I can feel the emotion in the room. I sent Les Brown two emails a week for six months outlining my story, what I want to accomplish as a speaker, and how he is going to be my mentor. **A:** Are you willing invest in yourself to attain your goal? I decided to attend a speakers training in Florida with Les Brown. **R:** What does this mean to you? I want to *Improve Mindsets and Elevate Vision Of Self.* **T:** Realistic and Flexible Timeline. My goal was to become a speaker by 2020; but I accomplished the goal in 2018, six months after sending all of those emails.

You must set your goals in writing. The physical act of writing your goals down makes it real and tangible. Be sure to use the words "*I will* or *I am*" instead of "*Would* and *Might*." I will or I am gives power to your goals. It starts the creation process. I would or I might lacks passion and gives you an excuse to not do. Make an action plan and list all of the steps needed to accomplish your goal. As you complete each step cross it off of your list. This shows progress toward your goal.

Remember to stick with it! Goal setting is an ongoing activity; you are in a race not a sprint. Be sure to set fulfillment dates for each goal. Never ever give in; sometimes people stop digging when they are 3 feet from gold. Find a mentor or a trusted advisor that has experience in the goal that you are trying to accomplish. Name a mentor or trusted advisor

_____.

Allow that person or persons to teach you the ropes. It's best to work smarter and not harder. Emulation is the highest form of flattery! Get Out There and Get It done!

Reflect~~ Release ~~Renew

Reflect:

What behaviors come to mind after reading this chapter?

_____

_____

_____

Release:

What behaviors are you going to let go of?

_____
_____
_____
_____

Renew:

How are you going to ensure you are not repeating the behaviors you have released?

_____
_____
_____
_____
_____

Day 15
Vision Wall

      A vision wall is a tool used to help clarify, concentrate, and maintain focus on a specific life goal. You can use images or words to represent whatever you want to be or have in your life. Most people like to use a board for their vision, I believe in a wall. My vision is too large for a board, I need a whole wall. Pick a wall in any part of your home and claim it as your vision wall.

When you add pictures to map out your destination it will become a 3D Vision Wall. Cutting out pictures helps to build the story of your life. Close cropping the words and pictures will create a 3D effect that you can use to walk right into your vision. Each morning and evening spend 5 minutes looking at your wall. Imagine how you will feel driving that new car or opening the door of your new home. Whatever your vision is you must imagine yourself living in that reality. If your vision is out of sight, then it is out of mind. Your vision must be in your face, so you eat, sleep, and breathe the story of your life.

Depending on what your life's mission is you can add subdivisions to your vision wall. Some of my subdivisions are Branding, Products/Services, Old Business Cards, Light Bulbs, Short/Long Term Goals, YouTube Playlist Ideas, and Affirmations. You might be saying woow, that is a lot! Well, I am pretty organized and it's important to envision the type of life you want. These subdivisions are mostly words on sticky notes, however you can do pictures if you like.

Branding tells me who and what my company stands for. I have my company's name and mission (Launching With Law| Improve Mindsets and Elevate Vision Of Self). I outlined the types of products/ services that my company will be known for (Speaking, Workshops, Coaching, YouTuber, Author, and Commercial and Print Modeling). The old business cards show me how far I have come. It also reminds me to trust the process and be thankful. Light Bulbs are my million dollar ideas that I date and write down daily. We have so many thoughts, any number of them could be million dollar ideas. I revisit them from time to time and try to bring them into fruition.

Short term and long term goals are what you want to accomplish now and in the future. I had a goal of becoming a professional speaker in 2020 and I accomplished it in 2018. You would then remove that goal for your vision wall. Be sure to include how much money you want to earn. I have checks on my wall from Oprah Winfrey, Steve Harvey, Ellen DeGeneres, and the Universe. Oprah, Steve and Ellen are going to give me a check for 50k for some type of partnership. Noticed how I called them by their first name, in my head, we're already friends. The Universe is going to bless me with $100k in sales for this book that I am writing, as well as $25k in unexpected income. How much unexpected income do you want? _____. Where it comes from is not of my concern the Universe just needs to provide it. Claim what you want and believe that it is already done! YouTube Playlist ideas are what I what to bring to life on YouTube (Law Speaks, Speaker World, Travel, Product Reviews). I envision my playlists as TV segments. When you are bored of one channel just switch to the next.

Affirmations are little statements that help to empower you. Thoughts create your reality and it's important to have positive thoughts. My second quote is "Money is Abundant, Money Comes To Me," this reminds me that when times get tough more money is on the way. I encourage people to say this quote when it feels like you have more month than money. Affirmations prompt you to consider your why, the reasons that inspired you to create the life that you want to live. Remember, if your why doesn't make you cry you need a new one. Did that rhyme (insert laughter)? Thoughts are your affirmations as well. What are you saying to self? Are those thoughts positive? Accept the negative thoughts and substitute them for something else. I substitute my negative thoughts with chocolate cake, I love chocolate! You can't get rid of the negative thoughts but you can replace them with positive ones. Replace your negative thoughts with whatever you love. My father loves Burger King, so he replaces his thoughts with Burger King.

Journaling is a great way to keep tabs on your journey and the thoughts within your head. Allow yourself to become one with the pages and express how you feel on the inside. It's best to journal on a daily basis, which is still a challenge for me today. Figure out what you want to write about or journal what is going on in your life right now. Writing about what is current works best for me, this way I do not get stuck on trying to figure out something clever to write about. You can also start off your journaling with the term "I KNOW I WILL BE SUCCESSFUL WHEN" and list 10 things. You can go even deeper by elaborating on the process of how you will obtain those 10 things. This will become your I's. Your I's are the goals or accomplishments that you outline for yourself. Create a list of I AM Proclamations and add it to your list of affirmations. Here are some I Am examples: I AM Successful, I AM Healthy, I AM Creative, I AM Infinite, I AM a Leader, I AM Worthy, I AM Deserving. Say it throughout your day and believe it! What are some of your I AM's?

_____

_____

_____

Reflect~~ Release ~~Renew

Reflect:

What behaviors come to mind after reading this chapter?

_____

_____

_____

_____

Release:

What behaviors are you going to let go of?

_____
_____
_____
_____

Renew:

How are you going to ensure you are not repeating the behaviors you have released?

_____
_____
_____
_____
_____

Day 16
What's Your Why or Reasons Behind Your Goals

Oprah Winfrey says it best "There's no greater gift than to honor your life's calling. It's why you were born, and how you become most truly alive." Your why is the purpose, cause, or belief that inspires you. Knowing your why will help you to find greater fulfillment in all that you do. We all have a why, you have to unlock yours.

There are 8 key benefits of knowing your WHY! **First**, it helps you to stay focused. It becomes easier to focus on what matters most in life. If you zero in on your goals it will provide you with a sense of direction and keep you away from distractions. **Second**, it makes you feel passionate about your goal. Your why helps you to find your true passion. Passions inspire you to achieve something extraordinary, e.g. a childhood dream or new lifestyle "Veganism." **Third**, it gives your life clarity. Your vision is clear and you become unstoppable. **Fourth**, it makes you feel gratified. When you have a purpose in life you express it often. Your decisions, thoughts, feelings, revolve around your purpose. I often tell my friends I can't hang out I have to work on the master plan. Creating a great impact will release feelings of gratification.

Fifth, it enables you to live a value based life. With purpose comes values and these values guide your decision making in life. Deciding between the right path and wrong path is a breeze (e.g. should I rob and steal?). **Sixth**, it makes you live with integrity. You are living a life that is true to your core values. When you live a life of purpose, you know who you are, and why you are YOU. There's no faking it, you are living your highest expression of self. I have an old keynote that says it best, "My Integrity is Defined By Me and Yours By You!" **Seventh**, it encourages trust! You trust the process and you will experience serendipity. Serendipity is good luck and valuable things follow it. Growing up I would always find money, it's as if it would appear right out of thin air. I am not talking about one or two bucks; we are talking about fifties and hundreds. **Eighth**, it helps you to find the fun and flow in life. You start to enjoy every minute of life. You find beauty and excitement in the dullest of things (e.g. cleaning the bathroom). You become one with the universe and you allow things to happen, rather than fighting against it.

Does your why make you cry? This is a recurring theme in this book! Your why keeps you moving forward and it's the reason why it must make you cry or at the very least get you emotional. What are you willing to die for? Is it a person or cause? These questions will help you to develop your why. What makes your heart hurt? Complacency makes my heart hurt. I have witnessed too many family members, friends, and neighbors become complacent in their situations. Growing up in the hood you see a lot of mindless souls just taking up space and not doing anything with their time. A lot of these individuals have a poverty mindset and never explore the world; let alone leave their neighborhoods. I implore you to find a why that excites you. Passion and purpose is a must. Passion drives creativity and it's the emotion behind your why. Purpose is your destiny; it's what you will leave behind. What do you want to be remembered for?

_____

_____

_____

Your why will inject passion into your work. If you know your why you will have the ability to inspire others around you.

Does your why wake you up in the morning? When you wake you should feel ready to take over the world. When you have a purpose lack of sleep isn't a bother. However, you should still get a good night's rest! Does your why fill you with pride? It will force you to share your vision with anyone who is willing to listen. Be mindful to guard your thoughts, what you think about you bring about. Every time my Pops (stepfather) would go to the mailbox he would always say another bill. If that's what you expect the Universe will deliver. After all, the Universe doesn't want you to think you are crazy. Bills after bills would appear in the mailbox. I told my Pops to imagine checks instead. Let's just say it's a work in progress. Your feelings are key in letting you know if you are on the right path. How do you feel most of the time?

_____

_____

You want to always feel good. Anger, hate, depression means you're going in the wrong direction.

How do you live your life? Most people live their lives on accident. They wake, go to work, cash a check, come home, deal with personal life, bed, and repeat. What a boring life; no wonder you are angry and depressed. Get fancy, figure out your why and dominate. Fulfillment comes when we live our life on purpose. You will find clarity and confidence in choosing the type of life you want to live. Associate yourself with relationships that empower you. Wake up inspired, Happy, and ready to go!

Reflect~~ Release ~~Renew

Reflect:

What behaviors come to mind after reading this chapter?

_____

_____

_____

_____

Release:

What behaviors are you going to let go of?

_____

_____

_____

_____

Renew:

How are you going to ensure you are not repeating the behaviors you have released?

_____

_____

_____

_____

_____

Day 17
BYE BYE Doormat

It's time to say BYE BYE to Doormat Syndrome!! As we discussed previously in Day 9, the definition of a doormat is a person that bends over backwards to please people. This term is mostly associated with women and men who are considered weak or wimps. However, I believe men and woman can both be described as doormats.
To rid oneself of doormat syndrome you must understand that it starts with you. Only you can elevate your level of worthiness! Here's a secret that we tend to forget "I MATTER MOST!" Everything starts and ends with me. Find a mirror or the reflection in your cellphone; just make sure you can see you clearly. Repeat after me, "BYE BYE Doormat." If someone is devaluing you, chances are you are devaluing yourself. Do you feel as though you deserve to be treated with respect? Do you feel worthy of respect? Giving yourself credit will raise your self-worth. You can do this by telling yourself how beautiful you are, what a great job you did on that project, or you look great in that outfit. You have to tell yourself sweet nothings. In the words of Ru Paul, "If you don't love yourself, how in the hell you gonna love somebody else?" Can I get an Amen!

You teach people how to treat you. Your response to someone's behavior teaches them what is and what isn't accepted. If you're in a relationship and your partner is cheating on you and you say nothing, your silence is approval. If you roll over and take what is given you are sending out approval. People will always do what's best for them and think about you second. Express how you feel so you command how you expect to be treated.

You are not a trash receptacle; if you take everyone's waste, I promise you no one will come along and empty you out. It's great to do things for other people, but not for acceptance. People pleasing is not a selfless act, it's a selfish one and it will always leave you empty. Beware of giving away all of your energy, it's not wise to take on everyone's baggage. This was a valuable lesson that I had to learn with family members. If I am everyone's rock, who is going to be my rock? We are all on a path and you have to allow that individual to walk their path. This is called Law of Allowing and we will dive deeper in later on in the book.

Questions to ask self: How can I be more generous with myself?
_____

_____

How can I please me?
_____

_____

Confidence is a must in saying BYE BYE to Doormat Syndrome and it starts in the mirror. Look in the mirror and tell yourself you're beautiful. Do it over and over until you start to believe it. Walk with your head high and look everyone in their eyes when you speak. Have faith in your abilities, "You're strong, you're wise, you're the best person to complete that task." What you see in people is a reflection of you. I often address anybody that I come in contact with as beautiful. It's a reminder to me that I am beautiful and I see beauty in the world. You might be thinking, "Will my new found confidence boost come off as arrogant?" It most certainly will not. Confidence is knowing your self-worth and that you are not better than anybody else. Arrogance implies that you are superior and better than all. In layman's terms your sh*t doesn't stink!

Remember you are not alone! There are plenty of people on this earth that feel abused and misused. Talk it out, lean on a friend or find a judgment free zone. Allow yourself to take a step back and gain a fresh perspective on your feelings. Have the mindset of fixing your problems. After all, God helps those who help themselves. This will help you to raise your expectations of self and the people you let in your circle. You decide what to put up with. If you are holding on to a toxic job, say *BYE BYE Crappy Job*! We are all about self-worth; consider the person you are becoming at that crappy job. If you are holding on to a toxic relationship, say *"BYE BYE Honey Boo Boo!"* You do not have to stay in that toxic relationship. You dictate how people treat you. The same goes for family members, say

"BYE BYE Family Member!" What people give is their karma and how you react is yours. It's not you it's them. That's where they are on their path; continue to walk on your path.

Welcome to the new you! You are Beautiful and wonderfully made. No more apologies, you are the best thing since sliced bread. It's time to live and not let time pass you by. Live like there's no tomorrow. Don't wait for the doctor to say you have 2 months to live. Expect the riches of the world and beautiful people to love and appreciate you. Live full and die empty.

Reflect~~ Release ~~Renew

Reflect:

What behaviors come to mind after reading this chapter?

_____

_____

_____

_____

Release:

What behaviors are you going to let go of?

_____

_____

_____

_____

Renew:

How are you going to ensure you are not repeating the behaviors you have released?

_____

_____

_____

_____

_____

Day 18
Count Your Blessings

    Counting Your Blessings is a phrase commonly used to remind people to be grateful for what you have! It's a reminder to think about how lucky you are instead of complaining. Each day you wake is a blessing. Are you alive? Can you breathe? Can you laugh, walk, talk, and smile? These are all blessings.

In life we often take the little things for granted. The act of breathing isn't easy for everyone. Watching my father struggle to breathe without his oxygen tank made me appreciate my lungs. Imagine having to be on oxygen for 18 hours a day or you will die. Not a soft pill to swallow. However, the good will always out weigh the bad. If your situation isn't the best find other blessings to focus on. How about that warm shower or fresh produce? Some people around the world do not have the luxury of taking a warm shower or cooking with fresh produce. Be sure to hold those close to you; your children, family, or friends. Be thankful for the bad because it teaches you how you want to live. Without the bad you wouldn't know what to appreciate.

How do you be grateful? You must be present in the moment. If you are at a family picnic or cycling enjoy the jubilation. Avoid being on your phone during family time, enjoy the laughs and make memories. Actively listening is important because we only retain 10 minutes of a conversation. When it comes to cycling enjoy the sensation. There's no such thing as pain. You are creating a master piece to look at in the mirror. Look for simple pleasures, there's positivity in all that you do. Before you close your eyes at night think of three things that you are grateful for. After each blessing say the magic word Thank You three times. This will prompt you to always be grateful.

Name three things you are grateful for.

_____   _____   _____ .

Do you suffer from WLS (What's Lacking Syndrome)? I learned this term from DoYouYoga.com. Do not focus on what's missing from your life; it will leave you in a state of wanting more. Lack just brings you more lack. You will not be happy if you just had….or if I can make this amount of money. You have to be happy now! You have to be happy with what you currently have and it will signal the Universe to give you more. Zig Ziglar says it best, "Gratitude is the healthiest of all human emotions. The more you express gratitude for what you have, the more likely you will have more to express gratitude for."

Health is the new wealth. If you have health you can do anything you want. I learned this valuable lesson after one of my hospitalizations. Imagine being in your 20's and not being able to leave your house because of a crippling mental disorder. Imagine other humans who are younger or more seasoned that have far worse ailments that prevent them from doing what they want. I am thankful that I am able to manage my disability.

Gratitude will always equal more blessings. You have to be thankful for what and where you are on your path. Understand that there are no mistakes; you are right where you're supposed to be. Every experience teaches you a valuable lesson to prepare you for greatness. Don't focus on wanting more; focus on being HaPpY and being kind to others. Treat others how you want to be treated. Have a serving mindset; help others for the sake of helping. Do not expect anything in return; God placed us on this earth to serve. Serving is the rent you pay for being on earth!

Reflect~~ Release ~~Renew

Reflect:

What behaviors come to mind after reading this chapter?

_____

_____

_____

_____

Release:

What behaviors are you going to let go of?

_____

_____

_____

Renew:

How are you going to ensure you are not repeating the behaviors you have released?

_____

_____

_____

_____

_____

Day 19
Self Development

Why self development? We face a variety of circumstances, changing environments, and new roles that require adapting. Self development helps you to handle the pressures of life. It helps to release the feeling of running into a corner in the fetal position. Self development is an ongoing process. You can't do it once and boom you're great. You must condition your mind daily!

There are four major reasons why you need self-development. **First**, it forces you out of your comfort zone. It will help you confront your weaknesses and be honest with self. You will experience growth and improve interpersonal skills. **Second**, it will develop your strengths. You will go from being good at something to being excellent at it. You will start to unlock your true potential. Be sure to focus and nurture those strengths. **Third**, it will boost your confidence. You will start to feel good about yourself. Improving skills and achieving goals with ease will cause you to know you are the bomb. **Fourth**, you become self-aware. You are taking an honest look at the areas in your life that need improving. Tapping into your value system will inspire you to get to know who you really are as a person.

The Secret on Netflix is a great place to start for self-development. The Secret was created by Rhonda Byrne and it's a self-help book turned into a film. It consists of a series of interviews designed to demonstrate the New Thought Claim. Lisa Nichols, Bob Proctor, and Jack Canfield are some on the many speakers you will see in the film. Lisa Nichols is a world-renowned speaker and creator of Motivating The Masses. She is the first speaker to take her company public. Bob Proctor is one of the world's greatest authorities on attracting wealth. Jack Canfield is a powerful motivational speaker and creator of Chicken Soup for the Soul. I love The Secret because it taught me how the Universe works and how to attract what I want into my life.

The New Thought Claim or New Thought Process began in the 18th century and it was only for the wealthy. The claim simply states, "when we change our thinking, we change our lives." This practical approach to life will result in increased health, joy, abundance, and success. You create your desired outcome. Steve Harvey says it best, "If you can see it in your mind, you can hold it in your hand." What you think about you will bring about.

Think and Grow Rich, A Black Choice is an audible book that I listen to at least twice a year. It was created by Dennis Kimbro and narrated by J.D. Jackson. The audible book demonstrates Napoleon Hill's Laws of Success and his vast knowledge of business and black culture. There are many black success stories; some of my favorites are Oprah, Spike Lee, and Madam C.J. Walker. This version of *Think and Grow Rich* was created in 1970 for Black America and it was completed by Dennis Kimbro. If you are looking for some self development on YouTube tune into *Be Inspired* and *Habits of the Wealthy*. These YouTube channels will condition your mind with positivity and substitute those negative thoughts. It will become your new music and you will find yourself repeating the affirmations over and over. *The Strangest Secret* by Earl Nightingale is a great read as well and it also comes in an audible version. What I love most about *The Strangest Secret* is the definition of success. Success is defined by self, whatever you say success is you must live up to it. If success is becoming a school teacher or a homemaker, then you are a success. Ensure you are the best school teacher or homemaker you can possibly be.

Be sure to avoid the news at all costs! The news is full of negativity and pollutes the mind. It's no wonder why most people have a bad day when the news is how you start your day. Why would you want to load your mind with crime, murder, pain and heartache? Yes, it nice to stay up to date with the world; but there are other avenues that you can use. Name one way you can stay up to date with world besides the news?

_____

_____

One of my favorite Zig Ziglar quotes is "People often say motivation doesn't last. Neither does bathing, that's why we recommend it daily." Self development is an ongoing process that will teach you how to deal with life. It promotes a toxic free life, with a focus on happiness!

Reflect~~ Release ~~Renew

Reflect:

What behaviors come to mind after reading this chapter?

_____

_____

_____

_____

Release:

What behaviors are you going to let go of?

_____

_____

_____

_____

Renew:

How are you going to ensure you are not repeating the behaviors you have released?

_____

_____

_____

_____

_____

Day 20
Law of Attraction

Law of Attraction is the ability to attract into our lives whatever we are focusing on; regardless of age, nationality, or religious belief. Law of Attraction uses the power of the mind to translate whatever is in our thoughts and materialize them into reality. Life is a blank canvas of possibilities and you are in control of the finished picture.
How do you make the Law of Attraction work for you? Follow these four steps.

1. Make Your Decision
    a. You need a clear vision of your desire
    b. Imagine that new thing with all 5 senses
    c. Imagine your life after receiving that thing
    d. You have to make it real in your mind
    e. This will prepare your mind and body for what you asked
2. Mange Your Thoughts
    a. If you do not believe you deserve what you are asking you will not get it
    b. You have to manage those fears and doubt (Fears are similar to radio frequencies)
    c. Weaken the signal or change the direction of those thoughts (Change the station, play another song)
3. Possibilities Are Endless
    a. Addressing your fears and doubt with acceptance
    b. Replace fears and doubt with appreciation and gratitude (Thank you for those thoughts, I choose to think this way)

      c. Fears and Doubt are just a part of the process, no guilt or shame

      d. Continue to practice Gratitude, be thankful for the process

      e. It's the key for setting you up for more things to be grateful for.

4. Experience The Reality of Your Desires

      a. Now it's time to live the desires you created

      b. You have to act as though you have it (If you want that new car go to the dealership and test drive it)

      c. You know what you want, you have to clear away all fears and doubt

      d. If you are releasing weight go to store and buy the size that you are meant to be.

      e. If you have a hard time finding a parking space, envision that car parked.

Your thoughts and belief systems send certain vibrations into the Universe. People that are operating on the same frequency are drawn together. When I decided I wanted to become a professional speaker I sent Les Brown two emails a week for six months. In those emails, I explained my story and how he was going to become my mentor. Les Brown became my mentor and he helped to train me. Vibrating on this frequency also allowed me to meet other motivational speakers and obtain a second mentor, Antonio T. Smith Jr. The Universe is a catalog and you can create a customized order. You can order whatever you like but you must order once! No take backsies on any orders. You must order it in a thanking manner and believe it has already occurred. The Universe is abundant and it will never run out because all humans do not want the same things.

My Order:

Thank You for...

    1. **I AM** AN INTERNATIONAL PROFESSIONAL SPEAKER

2. **I AM** A YOUTUBER WITH 1 MILLION SUBSCRIBERS

3. **I AM** A FOUR TIME BEST SELLING AUTHOR

4. **I AM** A COMMERCIAL AND PRINT MODEL

    a. (With Macy's, Old Navy, HM, Jockey, Nike)

5. **I HAVE** A Tooth Paste Commercial and **I AM** the First Male to be the FACE of ELIZABETH TAYLOR'S SPARKLING WHITE DIAMONDS

Thank You for my I's have already occurred!

A reoccurring theme in this book is "what you think about you bring about." All thoughts turn into things eventually. Creation starts in the mind and man brings it to reality. What are your I's? Please List 3:

1. _____

2. _____

3. _____

You are a human magnet; your thoughts and emotions will attract everything to you. If you are always happy you will attract things that make you happy. If you are always crying broke, you will attract ways to keep you broke. What you resist will persist and what you believe you will conceive. Now that you have an understanding on how the Universe works, create a plan and stick to it. Focus on your I's!

Reflect~~ Release ~~Renew

Reflect:

What behaviors come to mind after reading this chapter?

_____

_____

_____

Release:

What behaviors are you going to let go of?

_____

_____

_____

Renew:

How are you going to ensure you are not repeating the behaviors you have released?

_____

_____

_____

_____

_____

Day 21
Law of Allowing

Law of Allowing simply means saying Yes to Life! You are saying that you have no resistance to what you want and the flow of energy will be easy and direct. There is freedom in allowing circumstances to be what they are and people to be who they are! Law of Allowing completes the cycle of The Law of Attraction. You are allowing yourself to harness the power of the Law of Attraction and create an amazing life. Allowing the results to occur for you signals the universe that you are worthy of the gifts that you asked for.

Do yourself a favor and let go of the resistance! Mother Teresa says it best, "I Will Never Attend An Anti-war Rally; If You Have A Peace Rally Invite Me." The world has too much anti this and anti that, stop pushing things away. If you do not want something you simply focus on the things that you want to come into your life. The fact that the world places a lot of attention on the War on Drugs or No Smoking Campaigns, creates the energy of people wanting to be a part of that world. Letting go of resistance also includes letting go of judgement, resentment, and blame. As humans we tend to judge people based on their covers; your looks, appearance, and how you speak. Looking for the beauty in every human will help you to judge a little less. Resentment is a sensitive topic for me because I always want the best for people. I dealt with a lot of resentment toward Lady (my mother) because I felt she could have done so much more with her life. She has a lot of medical knowledge and she's a might fine cook. I learned from my yoga mentor that her greatest accomplishment was regaining custody of her children and finish raising them. Lady has expressed that this was her mission, but sometimes you hear things differently when someone else says it. When it comes to blame, you have to let go of what people have done to you and focus on what you want for yourself. I could have easily not applied myself because I grew up in foster care or drugs put a wrench in lives of my family. Stop making excuses and get it done!

Accept what life brings without judgement and understand that every experience is for your greatest good. There's a lesson in every experience that we can use to create the life we want to live. Do your best to pass the class the first time because you may not like the lesson the second time around. When I started to experiment sexually I remember not wrapping it up on one occasion. It was the scariest week of my life and I prayed every single minute. That experience taught me that everything that glitters isn't gold. I make sure I wrapped it up every single time, I probably wouldn't have been so lucky the second time around. That is not a lesson a I am wiling to retake! These experiences will help you to unlock creating your authentic self. Figure out what makes you Be (Highest Form of Self), How you think, What you believe, How you feel, and disregard what others think of you.

Remember to allow others to create their own realities. Allow them to be who they are and not who you believe they ought to be. For instance, let's say your parents want you to become a doctor and deep down inside you know that's not the life for you. Follow your bliss and become the person you want to be. People who often follow the realities that are predestined do not live a blissful life. You are your own unique self and you should express yourself as such. The same goes for relationships, some are meant to last a lifetime and others for a season. Learn what you can from that relationship and do your best not to hold grudges. If that relationship no longer serves you feel free to walk away. When you try to force or continuously repair the bonding you are not accepting the Law of Allowing. An ending always leads to a new beginning.

Empower yourself to embrace the Law of Allowing. You deserve supportive relationships and beautiful experiences. Attract more love, joy, and success into your life. If you vibrate at that type of frequency you will signal the universe to send you abundance. You are a magnet and you will attract what you are feeling on the inside. If you are always happy you will attract happiness. If you are always sad you will attract sadness. If you are angry, you will attract things to be angry about. You have the power to change what you are attracting. When you change everything will change for you. Say Yes to Life!

Reflect~~ Release ~~Renew

Reflect:

What behaviors come to mind after reading this chapter?

_____
_____
_____
_____

Release:

What behaviors are you going to let go of?

_____
_____
_____
_____

Renew:

How are you going to ensure you are not repeating the behaviors you have released?

_____
_____
_____
_____
_____

Day 22
Laws of the Universe Part I

In continuing the journey of the Laws of the Universe; there are 12 immutable universal laws that govern our world. The universe combines these 12 universal laws in order to create balance and harmony in nature. The most common universal law is Law of Attraction and Law Allowing helps to complete it. By no means are the laws listed below in sequential order.

The *Law of Divine Oneness* states everything is connected to everything else. What we think, say, do, and believe will have a corresponding effect on others and the universe around us. All of humanity and god is one. We are all connected by energy and the energy of god is all around. This is why we use the term "the god within me!" All objects emit electromagnetic radiation according to their temperature. Colder objects emit waves with very low frequency (e.g. radio or microwave), while hot objects emit visible light or even ultraviolet at higher frequencies (e.g. the human body). We should only think of each other as good. As you think of the good in others, they will in turn think of the good in you. You reap what you sow!

The *Law of Vibration* states everything in the universe moves, vibrates and travels in circular patterns. The same principles of vibration in the physical world apply to our thoughts, feelings, desires and wills in the Etheric world. Each sound, thing, and even thought has its own vibrational frequency. Like attracts like, as you choose good thoughts, more good thoughts of like nature will flow to you. This will cause a vibrational harmony among others with like thoughts. When I decided to become a professional speaker I started to attract mentors and other speakers into my world, because we were vibrating at the same frequency. Quantum physicists have shown that everything is comprised of energy and empty space.

The *Law of Action* must be employed in order for us to manifest things on earth. We must engage in actions that supports our thoughts, dreams, emotions, and words. You must do the things and perform the actions aligned with your purpose. This is when you will start to experience fear and doubt, but you must risk winning and continue to push forward. Tell your fears and doubts thank you for your concern, but I am going to go in this direction! If you wish to be anything in this world find out the steps to become it. Make a list and get it done!

The *Law of Correspondence* tells us that our outer world is nothing more than a reflection of our inner world; "as within so without, as above so below." The way you think and feel on the inside is a reflection of the way you act and experience on the outside. If you think negatively your outer world will reflect it. If you believe you are ugly your outer experience will represent everything ugly. How you see another human is a reflection of what you see in the mirror. I see everyone as beautiful because this is a fine piece of chocolate here (Please insert laughter)!

The *Law of Cause and Effect* tells us that nothing happens by chance or outside the universal laws. Every Action (including thought) has a reaction or consequence, "We reap what we sow." For every action there is an equal and opposite reaction. Every human thought, word, action, is a cause that sets off a wave of energy; which in turn creates an effect, whether desirable or undesirable. It's important to always choose good thoughts, words, and emotions to create your reality.

Reflect~~ Release ~~Renew

Reflect:

What behaviors come to mind after reading this chapter?

_____

_____

_____

_____

Release:

What behaviors are you going to let go of?

_____

_____

_____

_____

Renew:

How are you going to ensure you are not repeating the behaviors you have released?

_____

_____

_____

_____

_____

Day 23
Laws of the Universe Part II

It's time to complete the journey of the *Laws of the Universe*. Please use these laws to create the reality you want to live in. If my explanations are not clear, feel free to do your own research. There are lots of explanations on the web. Send me an email **law@launchingwithlaw.com** or tag me on social media @launchingwithlaw, together we can increase our knowledge.
The Law of Compensation is the law of cause and effect applied to blessings and abundance that is given to humans. The visible effects of our deeds are given to us in gifts, money, inheritances, friendships, and blessings. You are compensated based on what you give. You will receive what you give out; if you are kind you will receive kindness. If you take take take, you will receive nothing in return. Do more than what you're paid for and the reward is always greater!

The *Law of Perpetual Transmutation of Energy* states all persons have within them the power to change the conditions of their lives. Understanding this universal law will cause the energies of a higher vibration to consume and transform the lower ones. Your reality will change when you change; you are the deciding factor in all that you do. Nature tells us that energy is always in a state of motion (e.g. caterpillar turns into a butterfly). We can harness this energy and transform it into whatever we desire. Your thoughts are king!

The *Law of Relativity* tells us each person will receive a series of problems (tests of initiations/lessons) for the purpose of strengthening the light within. Each of these tests/lessons are challenges that we remain connected to in our hearts to help with solving future problems. No matter how bad we perceive our situations to be there is always someone who is in a worse position (#It'sAllRelative). Keep in mind nothing in life has meaning, except for the meaning that we give it. It's all about your perception of that situation. I could have allowed becoming disabled at 23 end my world. Instead, I learned the lessons that I needed to and I apply that to future experiences. Two of the lessons that I learned was to have gratitude and to not always want more. I had to learn to work within my means and be thankful for the little things. I am fortunate that I was able to work with my disability and become a stronger person.

The *Law of Polarity* tells us that everything is on a continuum and has an opposite. We can suppress and transform undesirable thoughts by concentrating on the opposite pole. It is the law of mental vibrations. You can't have a left without a right, an up without a down, the good without the bad, or failure without success. Learn to master, focus, and detach from the distractions of the materialistic world.

The *Law of Rhythm* states everything vibrates and moves to certain rhythms. These rhythms establish seasons, cycles, stages of development, and patterns. Each cycle reflects the regularity of God's Universe. Mastering this law means you understand how to rise above negative parts of a cycle, by never getting too excited or allowing negative things to penetrate your consciousness. An example of these rhythms are winter to spring or summer to fall. Energy in the universe is like a pendulum that goes from left to right or things that are growing and dying. This law also, governs our economy, health, relationships, and spirituality (e.g. the stock market has highs and lows).

The *Law of Gender* manifests in all things as masculine and feminine. It's the law that governs what we know as creation. The law of gender manifests in the animal kingdom as sex. The law decrees everything in nature is both male and female. Both are required to for life to exist. It takes a male and female to procreate. Everything has a yin and yang. We all have inner masculine and feminine energy. Feminine energy can be consider as giving, receptive, passive, and inward flowing. Masculine energy can be consider as taking, resistant, action oriented, and outward flowing

Fun fact: The only other way to create outside of the Law of Gender is to say Thank You three times before whatever you want or after you have received abundance (e.g. Thank You Thank You Thank You for the new car I am going to receive or Thank You Thank You Thank You for this unexpected income.) Three is the number of creation, which explains why it takes a man and woman to create and the baby makes three!

Day 24
The Secret to Life

What is the Secret to Life? Have you ever stopped and ponder this question? Did this question ever cross your mind? The secret to life is to be happy and do the things that make you happy. This might sound a little too easy, but it's as simple as that. The real work is figuring out what brings you joy and avoiding the things that take away your joy.

Once you figure out what makes you happy allow it to take you any and everywhere. Only do things that make you happy and/or bring you joy. I bet you are probably thinking happiness and joy are one of the same, however there's a subtle difference. Joy is an internal reaction to life. You have made peace with who you are, why you are, and how you are. Whereas, happiness is more of an external reaction to life; it is based on other people, things, places, thoughts, and events. I have accepted that I am a beautiful chocolate man with lovely dread locs. Traveling and spending time with love ones brings me a lot of happiness. It's best to live full and die empty.

What gives you joy?

_____

_____

_____

_____

What brings you happiness?

_____

_____

Create a balance life for yourself, the idea of balance may mean something different to each individual. When I think of balance I am referring to physical forms, emotional forms, and spiritual forms. All of which must be in alignment to prevent you from burning out in life. How can you have the energy to be happier if you're exhausted and miserable with life or from work? Do you have some type of workout regime? What type of internal conversations are you having with self? Do you believe in a higher being? I work out at least four times a week, to prepare for my sixties. The bonus is that I look good in my youth but I want to continue to look youthful. I make sure that my thoughts are always positive and I focus on what I am trying to accomplish. I am a spiritual person that picks and chooses what works best for me from any religion. I strongly believe that we are all connected through energy and that energy is the god within you. One of the most important things that I learned at Starbucks is *"Time Worked is Time Paid."* I implore you to leave work at work and home and home.

Time to dig deep and find clarity on why you feel the way you feel. This is the only way to move forward and truly understand your emotions. Say to self, "Why are we angry and sad all the time? What can we do to eliminate this feeling? Who or what is causing this feeling?" Once you have honestly answered all of those questions you will be able to eliminate people or things that make you feel angry or sad. In order to feel better about self, you must tell yourself *sweet nothings*. Tell yourself you are great, you are beautiful, and your life is abundant. Start to explore what happiness means to you. Does it mean taking that new job? Does it mean taking some alone time? Does it mean traveling the world? Whatever it means just do it!

When you are building your happiness things will change when you change! Your brain has a difficult time differentiating between your imagination and what happens in real life. You are what you say you are, so live within your values. Are you a kind person? Do you do for others? You can't go after life if you are doing the same thing over and over expecting a different result. Don't quote me but I believe that's the definition of insanity. Push yourself to go after your happiness and do it with urgency and enthusiasm.

8 Secrets to Life and What Society Doesn't Want You to Know

    I.   It doesn't matter where you went to school

          a.   Knowledge is the new currency

- b. Relationship capital helps to increase that currency
- c. If you read one book a month for 5 years, You will be in Top 5% of your field

II. You will be unhappy if you follow societal norms
   - a. Following your parent's dream for you
   - b. Time is of the essence, letting yourself down is a heavier load
   - c. Getting a job with good benefits
      - i. You can no longer work for 40 years and retire with a great pension

III. Happiness Trumps Money, but it allows you to eat better (Insert laughter)
   - a. Joy starts on the inside
   - b. You make the choice to be happy
   - c. Money allows you to make your dreams come true
   - d. Allows you to help others

IV. SOMETIMES PEOPLE ARE JUST MEAN
   - a. Don't take on that person's energy
   - b. Not your job to figure out why they are mean
   - c. A liar is called a liar because they are a liar
      - i. Read the story *The Scorpion and The Frog*

V. Do what you want
   - a. Create your own rules
   - b. We live in a world where anything is possible

        c. Figure out what you crave and get to the core of your being

VI. Think freely for yourself

        a. Society wants you to be a good little worker bee

        b. It's okay to question the system

        c. You do not need a pill to help you cope with life

VII. There's Always Time To Travel Travel Travel

        a. Travel turns you into a story teller, humans love a great story

        b. Life isn't about work, it's about your bliss

        c. Nothing in this world is out of reach

VIII.   Make time for nothing

        a. Schedule time to do absolutely nothing

        b. I'm talking you barely washed or brush your teeth

        c. Just be alone in a room with your thoughts

This is how you learn to love your own company.

Reflect~~ Release ~~Renew

Reflect:

What behaviors come to mind after reading this chapter?

_____

_____

_____

_____

Release:

What behaviors are you going to let go of?

_____

_____

_____

_____

Renew:

How are you going to ensure you are not repeating the behaviors you have released?

_____

_____

_____

_____

Day 25
Self Love

Self love means to have a high regard for your own well-being and happiness. Self love means taking care of your own needs and not sacrificing your well-being to please others. Self love means embracing the unconditional feeling of love, appreciation, and acceptance for you. Don't settle for less because you are the best thing since sliced bread! It's time to start loving yourself; you have to learn to be your own best friend. Sometimes we are our own worst enemy and self love helps to break down those walls. We have to embrace ourselves despite our flaws and our rejections. Bye Bye self-doubt, you can do anything that you put your mind to. You are great, you are powerful, and you are worthy. If you are experiencing self-doubt or low self-esteem, I want you to pick up your invisible sledge hammer and start breaking down those walls.

With my invisible hammer I am going to break down these four walls
_____, _____,

_____, _____.

Now that we have broken down some walls we can start to love self. I want you to find a mirror, the camera on your phone, or the reflection of a screen. Whatever it is just make sure you can clearly see yourself. Tell yourself how beautiful you are. Love all parts of your body. It's important to know how spectacular you are. You are wonder and beautifully made! Make sure you are doing this daily or any time you see a reflection of yourself. Often times what we see in the mirror is how we view the world. If you think you are ugly you will see others as ugly. If you do not have self love you cannot unconditional love someone else. I used to wear gray contacts for years and one day I realized how beautiful my eyes were and I stop! I had to learn to love all of me or none of me. That included my eyes, stretch marks from releasing weight, and my love handles (it's not as much as before, but I still have them).

Please let go of the notion of wanting to be perfect because it will never happen. Rather, focus on the journey of becoming your true self. Your mission is to get to being, which is your highest form of self. Everything is abundant and the world is perfect. All you have to give is love. This is why we are called human beings. You will start to process life as it is and not how you feel it ought to be. If you are going through a character building moment (bad times), accept it. If you are going through a sickness, accept it. Figure out the lesson and move forward. This is not the time to break down and say *"Why Me Lord?"* Why not you? Who would you wish it on? These are hypothetical questions, if a name comes to your mind you need to pray! Keep in mind karma does come back around; if you are wishing ill on someone it will come back on you.

Focus less on winning the approval of others. Be your own unique self. You do not have to do what everyone else is doing. Do not wait around for someone else's permission to live. Grab the bull by the horns and live on your own accord. Listen to your intuition and follow that inner voice. Allow your intuition to guide you in the right direction. Confidence comes from knowing that what you're doing is right and what you're doing is right for you. Trust in your abilities, all things are possible because you said so. There's a quote that I came across in the *Strangest Secret*," A man is success if he chooses to be." If your mission was to become a Housewife, well you are a success. You must give it your all every single day. Your reward is seeing your children grow into rock star humans.

Do something every day that makes you happy. Life is too short for you not to live. Invest in activities that you deeply care about. There's nothing selfish about self love. Experience life on your own terms before you can be life-giving to others. The best way to do that is to date yourself. Yes, that's right take yourself on a date! Get to know you again and learn to enjoy your own company. Go to dinner and do not feel bad about it. You must treat yourself how you expect your mate to treat you (#LawOfAttraction). I would often take myself to the movies with a packed lunch and a bottle of wine. I would spend a few hours in the movie theaters watching movies and enjoying my thoughts about the movie. Whatever activities you fancy take yourself on a date and have a good time.

It's okay to forgive your past self. Confront the dark parts of yourself and banish it with the light of forgiveness. Sometimes good people like you make mistakes. You are not bad it means you are human. Just as your forgive others you must forgive yourself. This will ensure that you Love, Love, Love yourself. People who love themselves come across as caring, generous, and kind to others. Self-confidence will start to ooze out of your pores. As you seek to understand yourself remember to understand others before you judge them. It's okay to appreciate the rude and difficult people. It's a great reminder of how not to be and that's just where they are on the path. We all have a path to walk and everybody is at different sections of the path. Everything will start to come full circle.

Reflect~~ Release ~~Renew

Reflect:

What behaviors come to mind after reading this chapter?

_____

_____

_____

_____

Release:

What behaviors are you going to let go of?

_____

_____

_____

_____

Renew:

How are you going to ensure you are not repeating the behaviors you have released?

_____
_____
_____
_____
_____

Master Your Choice In Intimate And Personal Relationships

Day 26
Complacency with Your Partner
Part I

     This is your Bonafide, Non-certified, Virtual Therapist Law Loadholt; here to rid you of complacency in intimate and personal relationships. The next four days we are going to dive deep into six universal habits that can help you to strengthening your relationships. Each day we will cover two main habits that have subtopics within each habit. Today's habits are *"You Get What You Give* and *Great Conversation Is Key."*

You Get What You Give

Relationships are hard, whether you're dating someone, dealing with friendships, or a spat with your mom. You have to be willing to put in the effort. Just as you attract what you want in life, the same goes for relationships. Sabrina Lawton says it best, "I know that the better I am to me, the better I'll be to others." You attract the type of relationships you want. You have to believe that you are an amazing person and so is your partner. There is no such thing as being half of a whole, another human cannot complete you. You will always be two individual persons acting as a unit. It's important to understand that you will always be your unique self; don't allow you to fall to the wayside side because you are in a relationship.

Are you always on the receiving end? There has to be a balance in receiving, you cannot always take and expect everything to be okay. You must learn to give and say thank you. Thank you can go a long way in relationships. It shows that you're appreciative for that individual's kindness and it doesn't matter how small the gesture is. Lack of appreciation can cause a rift or even breakup a relationship. This reminds me of folding my ex's laundry. I would take my time to make sure his clothes were nicely folded and he would unpack the laundry and throw into the dresser drawers. He would do this over and over, so I stopped folding his laundry. I decided to place all the unfolded clothes into the laundry bag. One day he asked "why I stopped folding the clothes?" I replied "I didn't, I stop folding yours because you didn't appreciate it." This could have easily become a tit-for-tat situation but he apologized and understood where I was coming from. In a relationship there is no such thing as getting back at each other, learn to talk about that issue and move forward. How you ever experience a tit-for-tat situation?

_____

_____

_____

_____

In relationships you must know your worth and command it. It's okay to teach your partner or friend how you want to be treated. If you do not like the way s/he is talking to you, you must communicate how you are feeling. One of the most invaluable lessons that I learned from my college professor,
Cassondra McCright-Smith is that you can't expect another human to think like you. It doesn't matter how long you have known a person, their thought process will always be different from yours. Do your best to find a common ground and solve the problem at hand. Abuse is never an exception, whether it is verbal or physical. If they do it once they will do it twice. If you feel combative toward your partner it's time to walk away. This was a clear sign that it was time for me to part ways with my ex. Our relationship could have gone down that route and nobody is worth me giving up my freedom.

Great Conversation is Key

How long has it been since you talked to your partner? Not the boring "how was your day or how was work?" It's crucial that you keep the conversation original. Act as if you're still getting to know each other and this will keep the flame alive. Keep a pleasant tone and positive outlook. Do not wait five hours to call or text a person back. You should be present for all conversations and if you do not have the time to do so, then just say so! Be an assertive communicator and clearly express how you feel on the inside. Get out of yourself and make it about your partner. Have a conversation about their interests or agree on a topic to discuss. Be sure to ask open ended questions like "What are three things that I do that you couldn't live without? What would you do in life if money weren't an issue? What is something that I can do tomorrow that will make your day better?" Name one opened ended question that comes to mind?

_____

_____

_____

_____

Try mentioning something you noticed about them "I love your hair, what made you consider that color?" These are all examples that will help enhance your conversations.

Practicing actively listening is most important! Be present in the moment because humans only retain 10 minutes of any conversation. Try repeating back to your partner or friend what they have said. This will create awareness and show that you genuinely care about their feelings. Give what you want in return and be present for all conversations.

Day 27
Complacency with Your Partner
Part II

This is your Bonafide, Non-certified, Virtual Therapist Law Loadholt; here to rid you of complacency in intimate and personal relationships. Our two main habits that we are going to cover today are Cultivate Romance and Recreation.

Cultivate Romance

It's important to keep the romance and physical aspect of your relationship in top notch shape. A lack of intimacy or distance over a long period of time is not normal. It's imperative that you figure out why the distance is occurring. Remember how sweet it was in the honeymoon stage? Well, that's where you want to remain. Get it on and make your partner feel wanted. The little things count most! Who doesn't want to feel thought of? What are some of the little things that you have done recently for your partner?

_____

_____

_____

_____

_____

Surprises are a great way to make your partner feel loved; consider a candlelit dinner or breakfast in bed (If you can't cook, do your best or just order out. Throw out the take out containers!). You have to take the time to express your love and appreciation. Rub their shoulders, foot or hand massage, or hold hands while you're walking. Whatever your deicide on remember to have fun fun fun.

Time to get sexy! Focus on what you adore, find beautiful, and appreciate about your partner. Create that affectionate feeling and let them know how you feel (e.g. Honey, I love your butt in them jeans or I love your smile). It's okay to clearly state your needs. Do not always assume that your partner knows you inside and out. Remember we are our own universe and we do not think alike. It's okay to feed your partner some bread crumbs. Be sure to express that you care about their needs as well. Embody self-trust and confidence. She or he is with you because you are all *"of that and a bag of chips."* You do not need to check his or her phone; all dirty deeds will come to the light sooner or later.

Five Effect Ways to 'Kill' Romance

1. Complain that the person isn't romantic to other people
2. Be critical often (e.g. You do not do this right or things that relate to manhood/womanhood)
3. Assume or project the worst before you have all of the information
    a. Listen to the full story before you assume the worst
4. Treat other women/men better than you treat your partner (e.g. Work wife or work husband)
5. Take things personal all the time
    a. Your partner is simply expressing how they feel
    b. This will build up a communication barrier

Recreation

It's time to have FuN fUn FuN. You have to spend time with your partner and do something fun on a regular basis. Take time out of your busy schedule and get it done. If you are that busy schedule it in, there are no excuses! This is how you create memories, those magical moments that you can look back on. Find ways to be active together, maybe a stroll in the park or working out. Some activities that you can consider are the movies, bowling, cooking classes, or sip and paint. Sip and paint is a great way to discover your partner's artistic abilities. Whatever the activity is just make sure you can talk about it years from now. What are some of your favorite activities?

_____

_____

If you are uncertain what activates to do together have a conversation and decide together. If you are still stuck here's a list to get you started:

1. Art Galleries or Museums
2. Take a road trip
3. Fair or carnival (release your inner kid)
4. Make Love, Yes get it on!!
5. Wrestle
6. Work on a project (e.g. home improvement)
7. Just spend time together

Day 28
Complacency with Your Partner
Part III

This is your Bonafide, Non-certified, Virtual Therapist Law Loadholt; here to rid you of complacency in intimate and personal relationships. Our two main habits that we are going to cover today are Intellectual Stimulation and Laugh Together.

Intellectual Stimulation

Intellectual stimulation is one of those things that are sometimes overlooked because we get caught up in beauty. You fall so deep for the person's appearance and then you realize your partner is dumber then dumb. I once dated a guy that was dumb and cute and I thought I could get past it. But, the more he opened his mouth, the more I knew it wouldn't last. Having intellectual stimulation will keep you interested in one another. Read a book or watch a documentary and discuss what you thought of it. Take a language course and have a secret language to speak. Get rid of the daily mundane routines and keep it spicy.

How do you know if you're intellectually compatible? Your partner should inspire you to expand your knowledge. Are you curious about art, literature, music, nature, or food? If you have a masters and your partner has high school diploma, chances are you will get bored of each other. Unless that person is well read. Level of education does not always determine intelligence; some of the smartest people in the world have not finished college. Do you have shared intellectual pursuits? You should only want to be with someone that inspires you to be greater. Once you have discovered the intellectual connection continue to nurture it through common interests. We are happiest in a relationship that causes us to grow based on mind, body, and soul.

Laugh Together

Laughter is a power medicine. Did you know one minute of laughter can boost the immune system for 24 hours? If you cannot make me laugh, we cannot be together. If you do not find me funny we cannot be together. I love to laugh and have a good time. Laughter helps you to overcome boredom. I implore you to figure out what makes you and your partner laugh. Maybe parodies, television shows, and movies are great start to laugh together. Consider stories of how you grew up. We all have silly stories of growing up that will make your stomach bust from laughter. My siblings are naturally funny and there was always laughter growing up in the Loadholt House.

Why is Laughter Good for a Relationship? Laughter helps to diffuse tensions. A dose of humor can ease the stress in a relationship. Forget about the silent treatment and try to find something to laugh about to regain communication. Laughter can help to regain intimacy. It fosters bonding and shows that you are comfortable with your partner. It can help you stay or fall back in love. You start to remember why you are with this individual in the first place (Yup, that's right he or she always made me feel this way).

Day 29
Complacency with Your Partner
Part IV

This is your Bonafide, Non-certified, Virtual Therapist Law Loadholt; here to rid you of complacency in intimate and personal relationships. Our two main habits that we are going to cover today are Make Travel Plans and Encourage Dream Catching.

Make Travel Plans

If you are feeling bored and complacent in your relationship consider taking a trip. Traveling could be the key to spicy things up. It's a great way to make new memories. Changing your location can change your outlook. Change the scenery, explore a new place, or explore a new land to bring you together. The fact that your partner is the only familiar face in a foreign land might cause you to lock arms. Who else are you going to trust? Have you and your partner consider taking a trip? If so where?

_____

_____

_____

_____

Taking a trip with your partner can help to eliminate distractions. There's nobody to get in the middle of your quality time (No kids, no work, no life excuses). This gives you time to focus on each other and the experience you are sharing. Try out new foods and explore the culture.

Lack of money is not an option as to why you cannot travel. Trips do not have to be lavish. There are lots of deals on Jet Blue Get Aways, Expedia.com, or point systems on your credit cards. You can organize a camping trip or a weekend adventure in a nearby city. Do two small trips and one large one to allow yourself time to save money. If your extremely hard up for cash consider a themed staycation. Do yourself a favor and tell everyone you are leaving the country and turn off your phone. Let's say you always wanted to go to India, learn all that you can about India and transform your home. It will feel like the best vacation ever.

Encourage Dream Catching

To have a successful partnership you must encourage each other to grow or you will outgrow each other. You must encourage each other to chase their dreams. Get rid of the *"should of-could of-would of"* that will prevent you from going after your dreams. Make a plan and get it done! Give the gift of validation and show your partner that their dreams and wants matter. Sometimes sacrifices have to made. For instance, lingering hours at the office for that promotion or getting that degree online or at night. There will be less time together but it will be for the greater good. In return you have a sense of appreciation for one another. This new venture will create excitement and create more conversation.

Here's some food for thought, no matter how long you have been in a relationship never assume things will fix itself. Always address all problems head on. If you want to keep your relationship and/or friendship you have to put the work in. Never lose the intimacy and always keep it spicy. Relationships are like a game of tug and war. If one party stops tugging, both sides will lose. Thank you for allowing me to be your Bonafide, Non-certified, Virtual Therapist!

Day 30
Wrap Up

It's Day 30 and it's a Wrap! I want to congratulate you on mastering a Choice Driven Life, you are the commercial driver in all that you do!! Thank you for sticking with this 30 day journey of becoming a new you. You are beautiful and wonderfully made who can achieve any and everything. You can continue your 30 day journey into the next 60 days by revisiting any of the 29 days you feel you are lacking.

The benefits of living a choice driven life are clear. When you live your life with a sense of purpose, you begin living positively and start seeking out new opportunities. You start to experience everything that you feel will make a difference in your life and the lives of those in your circle. Continue to condition your mind daily and focus on things you want in your life.

12 Pitfalls Of Not Mastering Your Choice

Day 1 *How I Could Have Been Complacent*

There were so many turning points in my life where I could have said "The heck with life;" growing up in foster care, feeling abandoned, not knowing my biological mother or siblings, becoming disable at 23, and dealing with mental health challenges. Sometimes life will deal you a character building hand and you have to play it to the best of your abilities. I will let you in on a little secret; there will always be another round. You are not your parent's mistakes; you can live a life of greatness despite your upbringing. I implore you to forgive so you do not live a life of hatred and anger. The world does not owe you anything because you were dealt a character building hand. You are strong, You are Bold, You are Beautiful, and you can make it through anything!

Day 2 *Do You See Life As A Learning Experience*

When you are not learning you are not growing. Your brain is a special kind of organ that acts like a muscle. It can be trained to improve different cognitive functions like working memory or math skills. Life is a never ending journey of self-exploration. I challenge you to figure out your purpose in a world of endless opportunities. Take the time to learn new things for self and/or your career. Whatever your purpose is in life use it to make the world a better place. Give meaning to your life by cherishing the experience and help others to realize their true potential.

Day 3 *Are Your Personal Relationships Suffering*

Poor communication is a clear sign that your personal relationships are suffering. Communication is the cornerstone of a great relationship. If you are always in an argument, maybe the issue is you! Do you always have to be right? Lack of presence can create a damper in your relationship. It's important to be present in your conversations. All relationships have a Reason, a Season, and a Lifetime. DO NOT BE AFRAID TO LET GO OF TOXIC PEOPLE!!

Day 4 *Never Feeling Nervous or Scared in Life*

If you never feel nervous or scared in life this is a sure sign that you are avoiding risk. Are you taking a chance on life? Are you risking to win by taking a leap of faith into the unknown? Flight gives you the option to run and fight ensures your focus on the task at hand. When you make the decision to succeed the world falls to the background and you're empowered to do any and everything. You must get out of your comfort zone to succeed in this new era of life. It's no longer about surviving you must separate yourself from the masses. Risk is a key element to success and failure is the only way to succeed. Failure tells you that you are on your way.

Day 5 *Fear of Change*

Fear of change is one of the most common fears that people face. People resist change because they believe they will lose something of value or control. There are 3 types of fear and 4 stages of fear. If you are implementing change remember to be compassionate and put yourself in the other person's shoes. Be the example of change that you are trying to implement. In order for change to stick you have to Expect the best, Prepare for the worst, and Capitalize on what comes. Whatever the change is look on the bright side and know that it will work out in your favor.

Day 6 *Taking Steps to Improve Yourself*

We can all improve on something; nobody in this world is perfect. The most important thing about improving yourself is self-image. When you look in the mirror what do you see? Spend time getting to know self; this will make you self-aware of your thoughts and what's going on in that big noodle of yours. An attitude of gratitude will increase your overall happiness and bring more into your life. Find a mentor if you want to completely elevate yourself. Follow what they are doing and add your own flavor. If all else falls pick up a book. You can learn so much if you read daily.

Day 7 *Are you Coasting in Life*

Coasting in Life means you are moving easily without using power. When you add life to the equation you are doing the bare minimum to get by. If you are just punching the clock you are coasting in life! It's time to lose the mentality "This is not in my job description." It's okay to serve others or go above and beyond without expecting something in return. Serving others is the rent we pay to be on earth. Hold yourself accountable and get it done. If you have to cut out the television or a get together to complete your steps, please do so! Your goals will become clear and you can easily measure your success. When you enter the workplace consider your mindset. The workplace can be your business or a company that you work for. Ask yourself who are you becoming? Are you happy? Do you feel successful? Are you excited? If you have negative responses to any of these questions it's time to plan your exit. You do not have to stay anywhere that does not serve you.

Day 8 *Taking Life and its Gifts for Granted*

Taking Life and its Gifts for Granted means to not appreciate or realize how much something really means to you. Life is so precious and you must cherish it every step of the way. It's imperative that you are thankful for the little things; your love ones, daily meals, and clothes on your back.

If you do not use your gifts god will take them back. Figure out your passion and purpose and use your gifts to maximize it. Passion is the emotion or why behind your purpose. Your purpose is what you feel you're destined to do or be on earth. Not using your gifts signals the universe that you are lacking gratitude.

Day 9 *Are You a Doormat*

The definition of a doormat is a person that bends over backwards to please people. There are five clear signs that you are suffering from doormat syndrome.

First Sign- Always apologetic (You are always apologizing for silly mistakes)

Second Sign- Playing the victim (Woe is me, everything always happen to you)

Third Sign- Expect to be treated poorly (You expect for people to use and abuse you)

Fourth Sign-Needs constant approval (Before you act you must receive approval from another human)

Fifth Sign- Always complaining (You're always complaining to others about the injustice in your world)

Day 10 *Financial Complacency*

Financial Complacency is not a strategy, it's a death sentence. If you have more month than money at the end of every pay cycle, you need a new strategy! Financial complacency is usually the result of consumerism. It's best to live by Zero Balance, a term that I learned from Dr. Shirley Davis. Make sure you account for every dollar spent. It doesn't matter how much money you make, it matters how much is left over. Money is a vehicle that works for you. You should never be working for it. Be sure to include yourself in your monthly expenses. If you have to physically create a bill with your name on it to ensure that you pay you, please do so! You cannot have the riches of the world if you do not pay yourself first. If you take anything away from Day 10 know that your millionaire and billionaire status is based on how much money you keep not how much you make!

Day 11 *Physical Complacency*

Many people may not know they are settling until the pains and aches of life start to creep in. The most common signs are disease, mental health challenges, and joint issues. It's important to be conscious of what you are placing inside of your temple. Your body is your temple and you must respect it as a sacred work of art. If you want to ensure your longevity on this earth you absolutely need a workout regimen. Working out helps to release endorphins, you know those happy hormones. They help to release pain and keep you in a state of euphoria. Mental health is extremely important to releasing physical complacency. You must monitor your thoughts and check your heart space.

There are six signs of depression:

1. Sad, empty, helplessness, worthlessness
2. Irritability
3. Less interested in activities (less meaning you loved an activity, but now it feels too tired some to do it)
4. Changes in your sleep patterns
5. Loss of Appetite
6. Aches and Pains

Day 12 *Forgiveness*

According to a psychologist the act of forgiveness is a conscious, deliberate decision to release feelings of resentment or vengeance toward a person or group who has harmed you, regardless of whether they actually deserve your forgiveness. When you forgive you are accepting the reality of what happened. You find a way to live in a state of resolution. It's not about the person who wronged you, it's for You! This process will allow you to heal and make peace with the reality of what happened to you. Why is forgiveness so hard? You're filled with thoughts of retribution or revenge. You might feel as though you have a moral right to get even, or maybe you just plain ol' want to get even, and it doesn't matter who. You think the act of getting even will make you feel superior to the person or persons that wronged you. Remember the four steps of forgiveness. If you decide not to forgive prepare yourself for a world of anger and bitterness. You will be unhappy, picking a fight for every little thing.

Day 13 *Forgiveness Part II*

Lack of forgiveness will lead a human down the wrong path. It will cause you to feel as though the world owes you something and you make others pay for the mistakes of the wronged. In this chapter I used my relationship with my father as example of how to forgive. Despite all of the ups and downs in our relationship I was able to forgive him and provide the care that he needs for his lung condition.

12 Ways To Master Your Choice

Day 14 *Set Up New Goals*

There are five golden rules you must consider before you establish a goal.

Five Golden Rules

1. Set Goals That Motivate You

2. Set SMART GOALS

3. Set Goals in Writing

4. Make an Action Plan

5. Stick with it

Make sure you set goals that motivate you. Your goals must be important and consider the value in achieving them. You must set your goals in writing. The physical act of writing your goals down makes it real and tangible. Be sure to use the words "I will or I am" instead of "Would and Might." I will or I am gives power to your goals. It starts the creation process. I would or I might lacks passion and gives you an excuse to not do. Remember to stick with it! Goal setting is an ongoing activity; you are in a race not a sprint. Be sure to set fulfillment dates for each goal.

Day 15 *Vision Wall*

A vision wall is a tool used to help clarify, concentrate, and maintain focus on a specific life goal. You can use images or words to represents whatever you want to be or have in your life. Each morning and evening spend 5 minutes looking at your wall. Imagine how you will feel driving that new car or opening the door of your new home. Whatever your vision is you must imagine yourself living in that reality. Short term and long term goals are what you want to accomplish now and in the future. Affirmations are little statements that help to empower you. Thoughts create your reality and it's important to have positive thoughts. Your I's are the goals or accomplishments that you outline for yourself. Create a list of I AM Proclamations and add it to your list of affirmations. Here are some I Am examples: I AM Successful, I AM Healthy, I AM Creative, I AM Infinite, I AM a Leader, I AM Worthy, I AM Deserving. Say it throughout your day and believe it!

Day 16 *What's Your Why or Reasons Behind Your Goals*

Your why is the purpose, cause, or belief that inspires you. Knowing your why will help you to find greater fulfillment in all that you do. We all have a why, you have to unlock yours. There are 8 key benefits of knowing your WHY! **First**, it helps you to stay focused. **Second**, it makes you feel passionate about your goal. **Third**, it gives your life clarity. **Fourth**, it makes you feel gratified. **Fifth**, its enables you to live a value based life. **Sixth**, it makes you live with integrity. **Seventh**, it encourages trust! **Eighth**, it helps you to find the fun and flow in life.

Day 17 *BYE BYE Door Mat*

BYE BYE to Doormat Syndrome!! The definition of a doormat is a person that bends over backwards to please people. To rid oneself of doormat syndrome you must understand that it starts with you. Only you can elevate your level of worthiness! Here's a secret that we tend to forget "I MATTER MOST!" Everything starts and ends with me. If someone is devaluing you, chances are you are devaluing yourself. You teach people how to treat you. Your response to someone's behavior teaches them what is and what isn't accepted. You are not a trash receptacle; if you take everyone's waste, I promise you no one will come along and empty you out. It's great to do things for other people, but not for acceptance. People pleasing is not a selfless act, it's a selfish one and it will always leave you empty. Beware of giving away all of your energy, it's not wise to take on everyone's baggage. Remember you are not alone! There are plenty people on this earth that feels abused and misused. Talk it out, lean on a friend or find a judgment free zone. Expect the riches of the world and beautiful people to love and appreciate you. Live full and die empty!

Day 18 *Count Your Blessings*

Count Your Blessing is a reminder to think about how lucky you are instead of complaining. Each day you wake is a blessing. Are you alive? Can you breathe? Can you laugh, walk, talk, and smile? These are all blessings. Do you suffer from WLS (What's Lacking Syndrome)? I learned this term from DoYouYoga.com. Do not focus on what's missing from your life it will leave you in a state of wanting more. Lack just brings you more lack. You will not be happy if you just had….or if I can make this amount of money. You have to be happy now! Gratitude will always equal more blessings. You have to be thankful for what and where you are on your path. Understand that there are no mistakes you are right where you're supposed to be. Every experience teaches you a valuable lesson to prepare you for greatness. Don't focus on wanting more; focus on being HaPpY and being kind to others. Treat others how you want to be treated. Have a serving mindset; help others for sake of helping.

Day 19 *Self Development*

Self development helps you to handle the pressures of life. It helps to release the feeling of running into a corner in the fetal position. Self development is an ongoing process and you must condition your mind daily! There are four major reasons why you need self-development. **First**, it forces you out of your comfort zone. **Second**, it will develop your strengths. **Third**, it will boost your confidence. **Fourth,** you become self-aware. The Secret on Netflix, Think and Grow Rich, A Black Choice, and The Strangest Secret by Earl Nightingale are great places to start for self development. One of my favorite Zig Ziglar quotes is "People often say motivation doesn't last. Neither does bathing, that's why we recommend it daily." Self development is an ongoing process that will teach you how to deal with life. It promotes a toxic free life and with a focus on happiness!

Day 20 *Law of Attraction*

Law of Attraction uses the power of the mind to translate whatever is in our thoughts and materialize them into reality. Life is a blank canvas of possibilities and you are in control of the finished picture. How do you make the Law of Attraction work for you? Follow these four steps. **First**, Make a Decision. **Second,** Manage Your Thoughts. **Third**, Possibilities Are Endless. **Fourth**, Experience the Realities of Your Desires. Your thoughts and belief systems send certain vibrations into the universe. People that are operating on the same frequency are drawn together. The universe is a catalog that you can create a customized order. You can order whatever you like but you must order once! The universe is abundant and it will never run out because all humans do not want the same things. You are a human magnet, your thoughts and emotions will attract everything to you! If you are always happy you will attract things that make you happy. If you are always crying broke, you will attract ways to keep you broke. What you resist will persist and what you believe you will conceive.

Day 21 *Law of Allowing*

Law of Allowing simply means saying Yes to Life! You are saying that you have no resistance to what you want and the flow of energy will be easy and direct. There is freedom in allowing circumstances to be what they are and people to be who they are! Law of Allowing completes the cycle of The Law of Attraction. Accept what life brings without judgment and understand that every experience is for your greatest good. There's a lesson in every experience that we can use to create the life we want to live. Do your best to pass the class the first time because you may not like the lesson the second time around. Remember to allow others to create their own realities. Allow them to be who they are and not who you believe they ought to be. Empower yourself to embrace the Law of Allowing. You deserve supportive relationships and beautiful experiences. Attract more love, joy, and success into your life. If you vibrate at that type of frequency you will signal the universe to send you abundance.

Day 22 *Laws of the Universe Part I*

The universe combines these 12 universal laws in order to create balance and harmony in nature. The most common universal law is Law of Attraction and Law Allowing helps to complete it. The *Law of Divine Oneness* states everything is connected to everything else. The *Law of Vibration* states everything in the universe moves, vibrates, and travels in circular patterns. The *Law of Action* must be employed in order for us to manifest things on earth. The *Law of Correspondence* tells us that our outer world is nothing more than a reflection of our inner world; "as within so without, as above so below." The *Law of Cause and Effect* tells us that nothing happens by chance or outside the universal laws. Every human thought, word, action, is a cause that sets off a wave of energy; which in turn creates an effect, whether desirable or undesirable. It's important to always choose good thoughts, words, and emotions to create your reality.

Day 23 *Laws of the Universe Part II*

In completing the journey of the Laws of the Universe, please use these laws to create the reality you want to live in. The *Law of Compensation* is the law of cause and effect applied to blessings and abundance that is given to humans. The *Law of Perpetual Transmutation* of Energy states all persons have within them the power to change the conditions of their lives. The *Law of Relativity* tells us each person will receive a series of problems (tests of initiations/lessons) for the purpose of strengthening the light within. The *Law of Polarity* tells us that everything is on a continuum and has an opposite. The *Law of Rhythm* states everything vibrates and moves to certain rhythms. The *Law of Gender* manifests in all things as masculine and feminine. **Fun fact**: The only other way to create outside of the Law of Gender is to say Thank You three times before whatever you want or after you have received abundance (e.g. Thank You Thank You Thank You for the new car I am going to receive or Thank You Thank You Thank You for this unexpected income.)

Day 24 *The Secret to Life*

The secret to life is to be happy and do the things that make you happy. The real work is figuring out what brings you joy and avoiding the things that take away your joy. Once you figure out what makes you happy allow it to take you any and everywhere. Only do things that make you happy and/or bring you joy. Joy is an internal reaction to life. You have made peace with who you are, why you are, and how you are. Whereas, happiness is more of an external reaction to life; it is based on other people, things, places, thoughts, and events. When you are building your happiness things will change when you change! Your brain has a difficult time differentiating between your imagination and what happens in real life. You are what you say you are, so live within your values.

Day 25 *Self Love*

Self love means to have a high regard for your own well-being and happiness. Self love means embracing the unconditional feeling of love, appreciation, and acceptance for you. It's time to start loving yourself; you have to learn to be your own best friend. Sometimes we are our own worst enemy and self love helps to break down those walls. We have to embrace ourselves despite our flaws and our rejections. It's important to know how spectacular you are. You are wonderful and beautifully made! Make sure you are doing this daily or anytime you see a reflection of yourself. Often times what we see in the mirror is how we view the world. Please let go of the notion of wanting to be perfect because it will never happen. Rather, focus on the journey of becoming your true self. Focus less on winning the approval of others. Be your own unique self. You do not have to do what everyone else is doing. Do not wait around for someone else's permission to live. It's okay to forgive your past self. Confront the dark parts of yourself and banish it with the light of forgiveness. Sometimes good people like you make mistakes!

Master Your Choice In Intimate And Personal Relationships

Day 26 *Complacency with Your Partner Part I*

This is your Bonafide, Non-certified, Virtual Therapist Law Loadholt; here to rid you of complacency in intimate and personal relationships. The next four days we are going to dive deep into six universal habits that can help you to strengthening your relationships. Each day we will cover two main habits that have subtopics within each habit. Today's habits are "You Get What You Give and Great Conversation Is Key." Relationships are hard, whether you're dating someone, dealing with friendships, or a spat with your mom. You have to be willing to put in the effort. It's crucial that you keep the conversation original. Act as if you're still getting to know each other and this will keep the flame alive.

Day 27 *Complacency with Your Partner Part II*

This is your Bonafide, Non-certified, Virtual Therapist Law Loadholt; here to rid you of complacency in intimate and personal relationships. Our two main habits that we are going to cover today are Cultivate Romance and Recreation. It's important to keep the romance and physical aspect of your relationship in top notch shape. Surprises are a great way to make your partner feel loved. It's time to have FuN fUn FuN. You have to spend time with your partner and do something fun on a regular basis. Take time out of your busy schedule and get it done. Find ways to be active together, maybe a stroll in the park or working out.

Day 28 *Complacency with Your Partner Part III*

This is your Bonafide, Non-certified, Virtual Therapist Law Loadholt; here to rid you of complacency in intimate and personal relationships. Our two main habits that we are going to cover today are Intellectual Stimulation and Laugh Together. Intellectual stimulation is one of those things that are sometimes overlooked because we get caught up in beauty. How do you know if you're intellectually compatible? Your partner should inspire you to expand your knowledge. Laughter is a power medicine. Did you know one minute of laughter can boost the immune system for 24 hours? Why is Laughter Good for a Relationship? Laughter helps to diffuse tensions. A dose of humor can ease the stress in a relationship.

Day 29 *Complacency with Your Partner Part IV*

This is your Bonafide, Non-certified, Virtual Therapist Law Loadholt; here to rid you of complacency in intimate and personal relationships. Our two main habits that we are going to cover today are Make Travel Plans and Encourage Dream Catching. If you are feeling bored and complacent in your relationship consider taking a trip. Taking a trip with your partner can help to eliminate distractions. To have a successful partnership you must encourage each other to grow or you will outgrow each other. You must encourage each other to chase their dreams. Thank you for allowing me to be your Bonafide, Non-certified, Virtual Therapist!

These brief summaries are all of what we covered these past 29 days! I implore you to continue to practice a Choice Driven Life! You are beautiful and wonderfully made. **Live By Law's Law:** *Living, Loving, Laughing, and Libations!*

To My Father

David Lawrence Caple

Forgiveness is one of the hardest lessons that I had to learn in life. I have been wronged by so many and yet I laugh, I smile, and I stand strong.

I often wished I could control the time we had, but no one has that power. I am grateful for the time we have spent. I am grateful for the lessons you have taught me.

Thank you for accepting the man I have become

Your Carbon Copy,

-Lawrence Loadholt

About The Author

Law Loadholt is a Transformational Entertainer, Leadership Coach, Keynote Speaker, Travel Vlogger, and Founder & CEO of Launching With Law. He's the creator of Master Your Choice Workshop and Releasing Complacency Training. He is trained by great mentors, such as Les Brown and Antonio T. Smith Jr.

Law's mission is To Improve Mindsets And Elevate Vision Of Self. At Launching With Law, clients are taught how to figure out their purpose in a world of endless opportunities.

"Life Is Choice Driven, You Are The Deciding Factor In All That You Do!"
-Law Loadholt

Follow the Launch:
YouTube: **https://www.youtube.com/c/launchingwithlaw**
Instagram: **https://www.instagram.com/launchingwithlaw**
Facebook: **https://www.facebook.com/launchingwithlaw**
Twitter: **https://twitter.com/launchingwthlaw**
LinkedIn: **www.linkedin.com/in/lawloadholt**
Tik Tok: **www.tiktok.com/@launchingwithlaw**
Medium: **https://medium.com/@lawloadholt**
Website: **www.launchingwithlaw.com**
Email: **law@launchingwithlaw.com**

Podcasts:
https://redcircle.com/shows/launching-with-law

www.ingramcontent.com/pod-product-compliance
Lightning Source LLC
Chambersburg PA
CBHW020248010526
44107CB00002B/156